YOUR
VICTORY
IN
JESUS

YOUR VICTORY IN JESUS

D. L. MOODY

WHITAKER HOUSE

Publisher's note:
The author's selection of Bible versions has been retained
whenever possible, including the Revised Version when
it was originally cited.
The text of this book, however, has been updated for the
modern reader. Words, expressions, and sentence structure
have been revised for clarity and readability.

Unless otherwise indicated, all Scripture quotations are taken
from the King James Version (KJV) of the Holy Bible.
Scripture quotations marked (RV) are taken from the
Revised Version of the Holy Bible.

YOUR VICTORY IN JESUS

ISBN: 978-1-60374-045-6
Printed in the United States of America
© 1995 by Whitaker House

WHITAKER
HOUSE

1030 Hunt Valley Circle
New Kensington, PA 15068
www.whitakerhouse.com

LCCN for the trade paperback edition: 2002011660

1 2 3 4 5 6 7 8 9 10   **W**   14 13 12 11 10 09 08

Contents

1. The Overcoming Life 7

2. Results of True Repentance 63

3. Let Your Light Shine 85

4. "Come Thou and All Thy House
   into the Ark" 107

5. Humility 133

6. Rest 151

7. Seven "I Wills" of Christ.....................175

About the Author 203

❧ 1 ❧

The Overcoming Life

*"Whatsoever is born of God overcometh the world:
and this is the victory that overcometh the world,
even our faith. Who is he that overcometh the world,
but he that believeth that Jesus is the Son of God?"*
—1 John 5:4–5

Part 1: The Christian's Warfare

When a battle is fought, all are anxious to know who the victors are. In these verses we are told who is to gain the victory in life. When I was converted, I made this mistake: I thought the battle was already mine, the victory already won, the crown already in my grasp. I thought that old things had passed away, that

7

all things had become new, and that my old corrupt nature, the Adam life, was gone.

But I found out, after serving Christ for a few months, that conversion was only like enlisting in the army. There was a battle on hand, and if I was to get a crown, I had to work for it and fight for it.

Salvation is a gift, as free as the air we breathe. It is to be obtained, like any other gift, without money and without price; there are no other terms. *"To him that worketh not, but believeth"* (Romans 4:5).

But on the other hand, if we are to gain a crown, we must work for it. Let me quote a few verses in the third chapter of 1 Corinthians:

> *For other foundation can no man lay than that is laid, which is Jesus Christ. Now if any man build upon this foundation gold, silver, precious stones, wood, hay, stubble; every man's work shall be made manifest: for the day shall declare it, because it shall be revealed by fire; and the fire shall try every man's work of what sort it is. If any man's work abide which he*

hath built thereupon, he shall receive a reward. If any man's work shall be burned, he shall suffer loss: but he himself shall be saved; yet so as by fire. (verses 11–15)

We see clearly from this that we may be saved, but all our works will be burned up. I may have a wretchedly miserable voyage through life with no victory and no reward at the end and be saved by fire, or, as Job put it, *"With the skin of my teeth"* (Job 19:20). I believe that a great many men will barely get to heaven, just as Lot barely got out of Sodom—burned out, nothing left, works and everything else destroyed.

It is like this: When a man enters the army, he is a member of the army the moment he enlists. He is just as much a member as a man who has been in the army ten or twenty years. But enlisting is one thing, and participating in a battle is another. Young converts are like those just enlisted.

It is folly for any man to attempt to fight in his own strength. The world, the flesh, and the devil are too much for any man. But if we are linked to Christ by faith and He has formed in us the hope of glory, then we will get the victory over every enemy. It is believers who are the overcomers. *"Thanks be unto God, which always causeth us to triumph in Christ"* (2 Corinthians 2:14). Through Him we will be more than conquerors.

I wouldn't think of talking to unconverted men about overcoming the world, for it is utterly impossible. They might as well try to cut down the American forest with their penknives. But a good many Christian people make this mistake: They think the battle is already fought and won. They have an idea that all they have to do is put the oars down in the bottom of the boat, and the current will drift them into the ocean of God's eternal love.

But we have to cross the current. We have to learn how to watch and fight and how to overcome. The battle has only just commenced. The Christian life is filled with conflict and warfare, and the sooner we find it out the better.

There is not a blessing in this world to which God has not linked Himself. God associates all the great and higher blessings with Himself. When God and man work together, then there is going to be victory. We are coworkers with Him.

You might take a mill and put it forty feet above a river, and there isn't capital enough in the States to make that river turn the mill. But get it down about forty feet, and away it works.

We want to keep in mind that if we are going to overcome the world, we have got to work with God. It is His power that makes all the means of grace effectual.

There is a story that Frederick Douglass, the great abolitionist orator, once said in a mournful speech when things looked bleak for his race: "The white man is against us, governments are against us, the spirit of the times is against us. I see no hope for the colored race. I am full of sadness."

Just then, a poor old woman rose in the audience and said, "Frederick, is God dead?"

My friend, it makes a difference when you count God in.

Now, many a young believer is discouraged and disheartened when he realizes this warfare. He begins to think that God has forsaken him and that Christianity is not all that it professes to be. But he should rather regard it as an encouraging sign. No sooner has a soul escaped from his snare than the great adversary takes steps to ensnare it again. He puts forth all his power to recapture his lost prey. The fiercest attacks are made on the strongest forts, and the fiercer the battle the young believer is called on to wage, the surer the evidence it is of the work of the Holy Spirit in his heart. God will not desert him in his time of need any more than He deserted His people of old when they were hard-pressed by their foes.

The Only Complete Victor

This brings me to 1 John 4:4: *"Ye are of God, little children, and have overcome them: because greater is he that is in you, than he that is in the world."*

The only man who ever conquered this world, the only complete victor, was Jesus Christ. When He shouted on the cross, *"It is finished"* (John 19:30), it was the shout of a conqueror. He had overcome every enemy. He had met sin and death. He had met every foe whom you and I have to meet and had come off victorious.

Now, if I have the spirit of Christ, if I have that same life in me, then I have a power that is greater than any power in the world. It is with that same power that I overcome the world.

Notice that everything human in this world fails. Every man, the moment he takes his eyes off God, has failed. Every man has been a failure in some period of his life. Abraham failed. Moses failed. Elijah failed.

Take the men who have become so famous and who were so mighty—the moment they took their eyes off God, they were weak like other men. It is a very noteworthy thing that each of those men failed on the strongest point in his character. I suppose it was because they were not on the watch.

Abraham was noted for his faith, and he failed right there—he denied his wife. (See Genesis 16.)

Moses was noted for his meekness and humility, and he failed right there—he got angry. God kept him out of the Promised Land because he lost his temper. (See Deuteronomy 32:48–52.) I know he was called *"the servant of God"* (1 Chronicles 6:49) and that he was a mighty man and had power with God, but, humanly speaking, he failed.

Elijah was noted for his power in prayer and for his courage, yet he became a coward. He was the boldest man of his day and stood before Ahab and the royal court and all the prophets of Baal. When he heard that Jezebel had threatened his life, however, he ran away to the desert and prayed under a juniper tree that he might die. (See 1 Kings 19:1–5.)

Peter was noted for his boldness, and a little maid scared him nearly out of his wits. As soon as she spoke to him, he began to tremble, and he swore that he didn't know Christ. (See Luke 22:55–57.) I have often said to myself that I'd like to have been there on the day of

Pentecost alongside that maid when she saw Peter preaching. (See Acts 2:14.)

"Why," I suppose she said, "what has come over that man? He was afraid of *me* only a few weeks ago, and now he stands up before all Jerusalem and charges these very Jews with the murder of Jesus."

The moment he took his eyes off the Master, he failed; and every man, even the strongest—I don't care who he is—who doesn't have Christ in him is a failure. John, the beloved disciple, was noted for his meekness; and yet we hear of him wanting to call fire down from heaven on a little town because it refused him common hospitalities. (See Luke 9:54.)

Triumphs of Faith

Now, how are we to get the victory over all our enemies? Turn to Galatians 2:20:

> *I am crucified with Christ: nevertheless I live; yet not I, but Christ liveth in me: and the life which I now live in the flesh I live by the faith of the Son of God, who loved me, and gave himself for me.*

We live by faith. We get this life by faith and become linked to Immanuel, God with us. If I have God for me, I am going to overcome. How do we gain this mighty power? By faith.

The next passage I want to call to your attention is Romans 11:20: *"Because of unbelief they were broken off, and thou standest by faith."* The Jews were cut off on account of their unbelief; we were grafted in on account of our belief. So notice: We live by faith, and we stand by faith.

Next: We walk by faith. *"For we walk by faith, not by sight"* (2 Corinthians 5:7). The most faulty Christians I know are those who want to walk by sight. They want to see the end, how a thing is going to come out. That isn't walking by faith; that is walking by sight.

I think the characters who best represent this difference are Joseph and Jacob. Jacob was a man who walked with God by sight. You remember his vow at Bethel:

> *If God will be with me, and will keep me in this way that I go, and will give*

> *me bread to eat, and raiment to put*
> *on, so that I come again to my father's*
> *house in peace; then shall the LORD be*
> *my God.* (Genesis 28:20–21)

And you remember how his heart revived when he saw the wagons Joseph sent him from Egypt. He sought signs. Jacob never could have gone through the temptations and trials that his son Joseph did. Joseph represents a higher type of Christian. He could walk in the dark. He could survive thirteen years of misfortune, in spite of his dreams, and then ascribe it all to the goodness and providence of God.

Lot and Abraham are a good illustration. Lot turned away from Abraham and tented on the plains of Sodom. He got a good stretch of pastureland, but he had bad neighbors. He was a weak character, and he should have stayed with Abraham in order to get strong.

A good many men are just like that. As long as their mothers are living or they are bolstered by some godly person, they get along very well, but they can't stand alone. Lot walked by sight, but Abraham walked by faith. Abraham went out in the footsteps of God.

> *By faith Abraham, when he was called to go out into a place which he should after receive for an inheritance, obeyed; and he went out, not knowing whither he went. By faith he sojourned in the land of promise, as in a strange country, dwelling in tabernacles with Isaac and Jacob, the heirs with him of the same promise: For he looked for a city which hath foundations, whose builder and maker is God.* (Hebrews 11:8–10)

And again, we fight by faith. *"Above all, taking the shield of faith, wherewith ye shall be able to quench all the fiery darts of the wicked"* (Ephesians 6:16). Every dart Satan can fire at us, we can quench by faith. By faith we can overcome the evil one. To fear is to have more faith in your antagonist than in Christ.

During the Civil War, Lincoln's Secretary of State, William Seward, a shrewd politician who had unusual foresight, prophesied the war would be over in ninety days. Young men in thousands and hundreds of thousands came forward and volunteered to go down to Dixie and whip the South. They thought they would be back in ninety days, but the war lasted four years and cost about half a million lives. What was the matter? Why, the South was a good deal stronger than the North had supposed. Its strength was underestimated.

Jesus Christ makes no mistake of that kind. When He enlists a man in His service, He shows him the dark side; He lets him know that he must live a life of self-denial. If a man is not willing to go to heaven by the way of Calvary, he cannot go at all. Many men want a religion in which there is no cross, but they cannot enter heaven that way. If we are to be disciples of Jesus Christ, we must deny ourselves and take up our crosses and follow Him.

So let us sit down and count the cost. Do not think that you will have no battles if you follow the Nazarene, because many battles are before you. Yet if I had ten thousand lives, Jesus Christ would have every one of them. Men do not object to a battle if they are confident that they will have victory, and, thank God, every one of us may have the victory if we will.

The reason that so many Christians fail all through life is just this: they underestimate the strength of the enemy. My dear friend, you and I have a terrible enemy to contend with. Don't let Satan deceive you. Unless you are spiritually dead, it means warfare. Nearly everything around tends to draw us away from God. We do not step clear out of Egypt and onto the throne of God. There is the wilderness journey, and there are enemies in the land.

Don't let any person think that all he or she has to do is join the church. That act alone will not save a person. The question is, Are you overcoming the world, or is the world overcoming you? Are you more patient than you were five years ago? Are you more amiable? If you are not, the world is overcoming you—even if you are a church member. In his letter to Titus, Peter said that we are to be sound in patience, faith, and charity. (See Titus 2:2.) We have Christians, a good many of them, who are good in some spots but mighty poor in other spots. Just a little bit of them seems to be saved, you know. They are not rounded out in their characters. It is just because they haven't been taught that they have a terrible foe to overcome.

If I wanted to find out whether a man was a Christian, I wouldn't ask his minister; I would go and ask his wife. I tell you, we want more home piety just now. If a man doesn't treat his wife right, I don't want to hear him talk about Christianity. What is the use of his talking about salvation for the next life if he has no salvation for this one? We want a Christianity that goes into our homes and everyday lives.

Some men's religion just repels me. They put on a whining voice and a religious tone and talk so sanctimoniously on Sunday that you would think they were wonderful saints. But on Monday, they are quite different. They put their religion away with their clothes, and you don't see any more of it until the next

Sunday. You laugh, but let us look out that we don't belong to that class.

My friend, we have to have a higher type of Christianity, or else the church will be gone. It is wrong for a man to profess what he doesn't possess. If you are not overcoming temptations, the world is overcoming you. Just get on your knees and ask God to help you. My dear friends, let us go to God and ask Him to search us. Let us ask Him to wake us up, and let us not think that just because we are church members, that we are all right. We are all wrong if we are not getting victory over sin.

Part 2: Internal Foes

Now, if we are going to overcome, we must begin inside. God always begins there. An enemy inside the fort is far more dangerous than one outside.

> *For we know that the law is spiritual: but I am carnal, sold under sin. For that which I do I allow not: for what I would, that do I not; but what I hate, that do I. If then I do that which I*

would not, I consent unto the law that it is good. Now then it is no more I that do it, but sin that dwelleth in me. For I know that in me (that is, in my flesh,) dwelleth no good thing: for to will is present with me; but how to perform that which is good I find not. For the good that I would I do not: but the evil which I would not, that I do. Now if I do that I would not, it is no more I that do it, but sin that dwelleth in me. I find then a law, that, when I would do good, evil is present with me. For I delight in the law of God after the inward man: but I see another law in my members, warring against the law of my mind, and bringing me into captivity to the law of sin which is in my members. (Romans 7:14–23)

Again, in the epistle to the Galatians, he said,

For the flesh lusteth against the Spirit, and the Spirit against the flesh: and these are contrary the one to the other: so that ye cannot do the things that ye would. (Galatians 5:17)

YOUR VICTORY IN JESUS

When we are born of God, we get His nature, but He does not immediately take away all of the old nature. Each species of animal and bird is true to its nature. You can tell the nature of the dove or canary bird. The horse is true to his nature; the cow is true to hers. But a man has two natures, and do not let the world or Satan make you think that the old nature is extinct, because it is not.

"Reckon ye also yourselves to be dead" (Romans 6:11); but if you were dead, you wouldn't need to reckon yourselves dead, would you? The dead self would be dropped out of the reckoning. *"I keep under my body, and bring it into subjection: lest that by any means, when I have preached to others, I myself should be a castaway"* (1 Corinthians 9:27). If his body were dead, Paul wouldn't have needed to keep it under. I am judicially dead, but the old nature is alive. Therefore, if I don't keep my body under and crucify the flesh with its affections, this lower nature will gain the advantage, and I will be in bondage. Many men live all their lives in bondage to the old nature when they could have liberty

if they would only live this overcoming life. The old Adam never dies. It remains corrupt.

> *From the sole of the foot even unto the head there is no soundness in it; but wounds, and bruises, and putrifying sores: they have not been closed, neither bound up, neither mollified with ointment.* (Isaiah 1:6)

A gentleman in India once got a tiger cub and tamed it so that it became a pet. One day, when it had grown up, it tasted blood, and the old tiger nature flashed out. Then it had to be killed. This is also true with the old nature in the believer. It never dies, though it is subdued; and unless the believer is watchful and prayerful, it will gain the upper hand and rush him into sin. Someone has pointed out that "I" is the center of S–I–N. It is the medium through which Satan acts.

And so the worst enemy you have to overcome is, after all, yourself. When a certain captain became converted in London, he was a great society man. After he had been a Christian for some months, a lady asked him,

"What have you found to be your greatest enemy since you began to be a Christian?"

After a few minute of deep thought, he said, "Well, I think it is myself."

"Ah!" said the lady. "The King has taken you into His presence, for it is only in His presence that we are taught these truths."

I have had more trouble with D. L. Moody than with any other man who has crossed my path. If I can only keep him right, I don't have any trouble with other people. A good many people have trouble with servants. Did you ever think that the trouble lies with you instead of the servants? If one member of the family is constantly snapping, he will have the whole family snapping. It is true, whether you believe it or not. If you speak quickly and snappishly to people, they will do the same to you.

Appetite

Now, take appetite. That is an enemy inside. How many young men are ruined by the appetite for strong drink! Many a young man has grown up to be a curse to his father and mother instead of a blessing. The body of a young suicide was discovered in one of our large cities. In his pocket was found a paper on which he had written, "I have done this myself. Don't tell anyone. It is all through drink." An announcement of these facts by the press drew 246 letters from 246 families, each of which had a prodigal son who, they feared, might be the suicide.

Strong drink is an enemy, both to body and soul. It has been reported that Sir Andrew Clark, a celebrated London physician, once made the following statement:

> Now let me say that I am speaking solemnly and carefully when I tell you that I am considerably within the mark in saying that within the rounds of my hospital wards today, seven out of every ten who lie there in their beds owe their ill health to alcohol. I do not say that seventy in every hundred are drunkards; I do not know that one of them is, but they use alcohol. So soon as a man begins to take one drop, then the desire begotten in him becomes a part of his nature, and that nature, formed

by his acts, inflicts curses inexpressible when handed down to the generations that are to follow him as part and parcel of their being. When I think of this I am disposed to give up my profession—to give up everything—and to go forth upon a holy crusade to preach to all men, "Beware of this enemy of the race!"

It is one of the most destructive agencies in the world. It kills more than the bloodiest wars. It is the fruitful parent of crime, idleness, poverty, and disease. It spoils a man for this world and damns him for the next. The Word of God has declared it: *"Be not deceived: neither fornicators, nor idolaters, nor adulterers...nor drunkards...shall inherit the kingdom of God"* (1 Corinthians 6:9–10).

How can we overcome the enemy? Bitter experience proves that man is not powerful enough in his own strength. The only cure for the accursed appetite is regeneration, a new life, the power of the risen Christ within us. Let a man who is given to strong drink look to God for help, and He will give him victory over his appetite. Jesus Christ came to destroy the works of the devil, and He will take away that appetite, if you will let Him.

Temper

Then, there is temper. I wouldn't give much for a man who has no temper. Steel isn't good for anything if it doesn't have temper. But when temper gets the mastery over me, I am its slave, and it is a source of weakness. It may be made a great power for good all through my life and help me, or it may become my greatest enemy from within and rob me of power. The current in some rivers is so strong as to make them useless for navigation.

Someone has said that a preacher will never fail to reach people when he speaks of temper. It is astonishing how little mastery even professing Christians have over it. A friend of mine in England was out visiting and, while sitting in the parlor, heard an awful noise in the hall. He asked what it meant and was told that it was only the doctor throwing his boots downstairs because they were not properly polished. "Many Christians," said an old theologian, "who bore the loss of a child or of all their property with the most heroic Christian fortitude, are entirely vanquished by the breaking of a dish or the blunders of a servant."

I have had people say to me, "Mr. Moody, how can I get control of my temper?"

If you really want to get control, I will tell you how, but you won't like the medicine. Treat it as a sin, and confess it. People look upon it as a misfortune, and one lady told me she inherited it from her father and mother. Suppose she did. That is no excuse for her.

When you realize that you've gotten angry or spoken unkindly to a person, go and ask that person to forgive you. You won't get mad at that person for twenty-four hours. You might get mad in about forty-eight hours, but go the second time. After you have done it about half a dozen times, you will get out of the business, because it makes the old flesh burn.

A lady said to me once, "I have got so in the habit of exaggerating that my friends accuse me of exaggerating so much so that they don't understand me."

She asked, "Can you help me? What can I do to overcome it?"

"Well," I said, "the next time you catch yourself lying, go right to that party and say you have lied, and tell him you are sorry. Say it is a lie; stamp it out, root and branch; that is what you want to do."

"Oh," she said, "I wouldn't like to call it lying." But that is what it was.

Christianity isn't worth a snap of your fingers if it doesn't straighten out your character. I have gotten tired of all mere gush and sentiment. If people can't tell when you are telling the truth, there is something radically wrong, and you had better straighten it out right away. Now, are you ready to do it? Bring yourself to it, whether you want to or not.

Have you found someone who has been offended by something you have done? Go right to him and tell him you are sorry. You say you are not to blame. Never mind; go right to him, and tell him you are sorry. I have had to do it a good many times. An impulsive man like myself has to do it often, but I sleep all the more sweetly at night when I get things straightened out. Confession never fails to bring a blessing.

I have sometimes had to get off the platform and go down to ask a man's forgiveness before I could go on preaching. A Christian man ought to be a gentleman all the time, but if he is not and finds he has wounded or hurt someone, he ought to go and straighten it out at once.

You know, there are a great many people who want just enough Christianity to make them respectable. They don't think about this overcoming life that gets the victory all the time. They have their blue days and their cross days, and their children say, "Mother is cross today, and you will have to be very careful."

We don't want any of these touchy, blue days, these ups and downs. If we are overcoming, this is the effect our life is going to have on others: They will have confidence in our Christianity. The reason that many men have no power is that there is some cursed sin covered up. There will not be a drop of dew until that sin is brought to light. Get right inside. We can go out like giants and conquer the world if everything is right within.

Paul said that we are to be sound in faith, in patience, and in love. (See Titus 2:2.) If a man is unsound in his faith, the clergy take the ecclesiastical sword and cut him off at once. But he may be ever so unsound in charity or in patience, and nothing is said about that. We must be sound in faith, in love, and in patience if we are going to be true to God.

How delightful it is to meet a man who can control his temper! It was said of Wilberforce that a friend once found him in the greatest agitation, looking for a dispatch he had mislaid for which one of the royal family was waiting. Just then, as if to make it still more trying, a disturbance was heard in the nursery.

"Now," thought the friend, "surely his temper will give way."

The thought had hardly passed through his mind when Wilberforce turned to him and said, "What a blessing it is to hear those dear children! Only think what a relief, among other hurries, to hear their voices and know they are well."

Covetousness

Take the sin of covetousness. There is more said in the Bible against it than against drunkenness. I must get it out of me—destroy it, root and branch, and not let it have dominion over me.

We think that a man who gets drunk is a horrid monster, but a covetous man, who is as vile and black in the sight of God as any drunkard, will often be received into the church and put into office.

The most dangerous thing about this sin is that it is not generally regarded as very heinous. Of course, we all have contempt for misers, but all covetous men are not misers. Another thing to note about it is that it often fastens upon the old rather than upon the young.

Let's see what the Bible says about covetousness:

> *Mortify therefore your members which are upon the earth; fornication, uncleanness, inordinate affection, evil concupiscence, and covetousness, which is idolatry.* (Colossians 3:5)

> *No...covetous man, who is an idolater, hath any inheritance in the kingdom of Christ and of God.*
> (Ephesians 5:5)

> *They that will be* [that is, desire to be] *rich fall into temptation and a snare, and into many foolish and hurtful lusts, which drown men in destruction and perdition. For the love of money is the root of all evil: which while some coveted after, they have erred from the faith, and pierced themselves through with many sorrows.* (1 Timothy 6:9–10)

> *The wicked...blesseth the covetous, whom the LORD abhorreth.*
> (Psalm 10:3)

Covetousness enticed Lot into Sodom. It caused the destruction of Achan and all his house. It was the iniquity of Balaam. It was the sin of Samuel's sons. It left Gehazi a leper. It sent the rich young ruler away sorrowful. It led Judas to sell his Master and Lord. It brought about the death of Ananias and Sapphira. It was the blot in the character of Felix. What victims it has had in all ages!

Do you say, "How am I going to check covetousness?"

Well, I don't think there is any difficulty about that. If you find yourself getting very covetous, very miserly, wanting to get everything you can into your possession—just say to covetousness that you will strangle it and rid it out of your disposition.

A wealthy farmer in the state of New York, who had been a noted miser and a very selfish man, was converted. Soon after his conversion, a poor man, who had been burned out and had no provisions, came to him one day to ask for help. This young convert thought he would be liberal and give him a ham from his smokehouse. He started toward the smokehouse, and, on the way, the tempter said, "Give him the smallest one you have."

He struggled all the way as to whether he would give a large or a small one. In order to overcome his selfishness, he took down the biggest ham and gave it to the man.

The tempter said, "You are a fool."

But he replied, "If you don't keep still, I will give him every ham I have in the smokehouse."

If you find that you are selfish, give something. Determine to overcome that spirit of selfishness and to keep your body under, no matter what it may cost.

William Durant told me that he was engaged by Goodyear to defend the rubber patent, and he was to have half of the money that came from the patent if he succeeded. One day he woke up to find that he was a rich man. He said that the greatest struggle of his life then took place as to whether he would let money be his master or whether he would be master of money, whether he would be its slave or make it a slave to him. At last he got the victory, and that is how Wellesley College was built.

Are You Jealous or Envious?

Go and do a good turn for that person of whom you are jealous. That is the way to cure jealousy; it will kill it. Jealousy is a devil; it is a horrid monster. The poets imagined that Envy dwelled in a dark cave, being pale and thin, scrunching up his eyes, never rejoicing except in the misfortune of others, and hurting himself continually.

There is a fable of an eagle that could outfly another, and the other didn't like it. The latter was with a sportsman one day and said to him, "I wish you would bring down that eagle."

The sportsman replied that he would if he only had some feathers to put into the arrow. So the eagle pulled one out of his wing. The arrow was shot but didn't quite reach the rival eagle; it was flying too high. The envious eagle pulled out more feathers and kept pulling them out until he lost so many that he couldn't fly, and then the sportsman turned around and killed him. My friend, if you are jealous, the only man you can hurt is yourself.

There were two businessmen, both merchants, and there was great rivalry between them, a great deal of bitter feeling. One of them was converted. He went to his minister and said, "I am still jealous of that man, and I do not know how to overcome it."

"Well," the minister said, "if a man comes into your store to buy goods, and you cannot supply him, just send him over to your neighbor."

He said he wouldn't like to do that. "Well," the minister said, "you do it and you will kill jealousy."

He said he would, and when a customer came into his store for goods that he did not have, he would tell him to go across the street to his neighbor's.

By and by, the other began to send his customers over to this man's store, and the breach was healed.

Pride

Then, there is pride. This is another one of those sins that the Bible so strongly condemns but that the world hardly reckons as a sin at all. *"An high look, and a proud heart...is sin"* (Proverbs 21:4). *"Every one that is proud in heart is an abomination to the Lord: though hand join in hand, he shall not be unpunished"* (Proverbs 16:5). Christ included pride among those evil things that, proceeding out of the heart of a man, defile him.

People have an idea that it is just the wealthy who are proud. But go down to some of the back streets, and you will find that some of the very poorest are as proud as the richest. It is the heart, you know. People who don't have any money are just as proud as those who do have it. We have to crush it out. It is an enemy.

You needn't be proud of your face, for there is not one that, after ten days in the grave, the worms will not be eating. There is nothing to be proud of, is there? Let us ask God to deliver us from pride.

You can't fold your arms and say, "Lord, take pride out of me." Instead, just go and work with Him. Mortify your pride by cultivating humility. *"Put on therefore,"* Paul said, *"as the elect of God, holy and beloved...humbleness of mind"* (Colossians 3:12). *"Be clothed with humility,"* Peter said in 1 Peter 5:5. *"Blessed are the poor in spirit"* (Matthew 5:3).

Part 3: External Foes

What are our enemies outside of us? What did James say? *"Know ye not that the friendship of the world is enmity with God? whosoever therefore will be a friend of the world is the enemy of God"* (James 4:4). And John? *"Love not the world, neither the things that are in the world. If any man love the world, the love of the Father is not in him"* (1 John 2:15).

Now, people want to know what the world is. When you talk with them, they say, "Well, when you say 'the world,' what do you mean?"

Here we have the answer in the next verses:

For all that is in the world, the lust of the flesh, and the lust of the eyes, and the pride of life, is not of the Father, but is of the world. And the world passeth away, and the lust thereof: but he that doeth the will of God abideth for ever.

(1 John 2:16–17)

"The world" does not mean nature around us; God nowhere tells us that the material world is an enemy to be overcome. On the contrary, we read, *"The earth is the* Lord's, *and the fulness thereof; the world, and they that dwell therein"* (Psalm 24:1). *"The heavens declare the glory of God; and the firmament showeth his handiwork"* (Psalm 19:1).

The world refers to human life and society as far as they are alienated from God—through being centered on material aims and objects—and thus opposed to God's Spirit and kingdom. Christ said,

If the world hate you, ye know that it hated me before it hated you....I have given them thy word; and the world hath hated them, because

42

they are not of the world, even as I am not of the world.

(John 15:18, 17:14)

Love of the world means the forgetfulness of an eternal future for the love for passing things.

How can the world be overcome? Not by education, not by experience—only by faith.

This is the victory that overcometh the world, even our faith. Who is he that overcometh the world, but he that believeth that Jesus is the Son of God? (1 John 5:4–5)

Worldly Habits and Fashions

We must fight worldly habits and fashions. We must often go against the customs of the world. I have great respect for a man who can stand up against all the world for what he believes is right. He who can stand alone is a hero.

Suppose it is the custom for young men to do certain things that you wouldn't like your mother to know of—things that your mother taught you are wrong. You may have to stand up alone among all your companions.

They will say, "You can't get away from your mother, eh? Tied to your mother's apron strings!"

But you just say, "Yes! I have some respect for my mother. She taught me what is right, and she is the best friend I have. I believe that this is wrong, and I am going to stand for the right." If you have to stand alone, stand. Enoch did it, and Joseph and Elisha and Paul. God has kept such men in all ages.

Someone says, "I move in society where they have wine parties. I know it is rather a dangerous thing because my son is apt to follow me. But I can stop whenever I want to; perhaps my son doesn't have the same power that I have, and he may go over the dam. But it is the custom in the society in which I move."

Once, I got into a place where I had to get up and leave. I was invited into a home. They had a late supper, and there were seven kinds of liquor on the table. I am ashamed to say they were Christian people. A deacon urged a young lady to drink until her face flushed. I rose from the table and went out; I felt that it was no place for me. They considered me very rude. That was going against custom; that was entering a protest against such an infernal thing. Let us go against custom when it leads people astray.

I was told in a southern college, some years ago, that no man who did not drink was considered a first-class gentleman. Of course, it is not so now.

Pleasure

Another enemy is worldly pleasure. A great many people are just drowned in pleasure. They have no time for any meditation at all. Many a man has been lost to society and lost to his family by giving himself up to the god of pleasure. God wants His children to be happy but in a way that will help and not hinder them.

A lady came to me once and said, "Mr. Moody, I wish you would tell me how I can become a Christian." The tears were rolling down her cheeks, and she was in a very favorable mood to hear God's word. "But," she said, "I don't want to be one of your kind."

"Well," I asked, "have I got any particular kind? What is the matter with my Christianity?"

"Well," she said, "my father was a doctor and had a large practice, and he used to get so tired that he used to take us to the theater. We were a large family of girls, and we had tickets for theaters three or four times a week. I suppose we were there a good deal oftener than we were in church. I am married to a lawyer, and he has a large practice. He gets so tired that he takes us out to the theater." And she said, "I am far better acquainted with the theater and theater people than with the church and church people, and I don't want to give up the theater."

"Well," I said, "did you ever hear me say anything about theaters? There have been reporters here every day for all the different papers, and they are giving my sermons verbatim in one paper. Have you ever seen anything in the sermons against the theaters?"

She said, "No."

"Well," I said, "I have seen you in the audience every afternoon for several weeks, and have you heard me say anything against theaters?"

No, she hadn't.

"Well," I said, "what made you bring this up?"

"Why, I supposed you didn't believe in theaters."

"What made you think that?"

"Why," she said, "do you ever go?"

"No."

"Why don't you go?"

"Because I have something better. I would sooner go out into the street and eat dirt than do some of the things I used to do before I became a Christian."

"Why?" she said. "I don't understand."

"Never mind," I said. "When Jesus Christ has all the preeminence, you will understand it all. He didn't come down here and say we shouldn't go here and we shouldn't go there, and lay down a lot of rules; but He laid down great principles. Now, He says if you love Him, you will take delight in pleasing Him." And I began to preach Christ to her.

The tears started again. She said, "I tell you, Mr. Moody, that sermon on the indwelling of Christ yesterday afternoon just broke my heart. I admire Him, and I want to be a Christian, but I don't want to give up the theaters."

I said, "Please don't mention them again. I don't want to talk about theaters. I want to talk to you about Christ." So I took my Bible, and I read to her about Christ.

But she said again, "Mr. Moody, can I go to the theater if I become a Christian?"

"Yes," I said, "you can go to the theater just as much as you like if you are a real, true Christian and can go with His blessing."

"Well," she said, "I am glad you are not so narrow-minded as some."

She felt quite relieved to think that she could go to the theaters and be a Christian. But I said, "If you can go to the theater for the glory of God, keep on going; only be sure that you go for the glory of God. If you are a Christian, you will be glad to do whatever will please Him."

I really think she became a Christian that day. The burden had gone. There was joy. But just as she was leaving me at the door, she said, "I am not going to give up the theater."

In a few days she came back to me and said, "Mr. Moody, I understand all about that theater business now. I went the other night. There was a large party at our house, and my husband wanted us to go, and we went. But when the curtain lifted, everything looked so different. I said to my husband, 'This is no place for me; this is horrible. I am not going to stay here. I am going home.' He said, 'Don't make a fool of yourself. Everyone has heard that you have been converted in the Moody meetings, and if you go out, it will be all through fashionable society. I beg of you, don't make a fool of yourself by getting up and going out.' But I said, 'I have been making a fool of myself all my life.'"

Now, the theater hadn't changed, but she had something better and was going to overcome the world. *"They that are after the flesh do mind the things of the flesh; but they that are after the Spirit the things of the Spirit"* (Romans 8:5). When Christ has the first place in your heart, you are going to get victory. Just do whatever you know will please Him. The great objection I have to worldly things is that they get the mastery and become a hindrance to spiritual growth.

Business

It may be that we have to overcome in business. Perhaps it is business morning, noon, and night, and Sundays, too. When a man will drive like Jehu all the week and like a snail on Sunday, isn't there something wrong with him? (See 2 Kings 9.) Now, business is legitimate, and a man who will not go out and earn his bread by the sweat of his brow is not, I think, a good citizen. He ought to be a good businessman, and whatever he does, do it thoroughly. At the same time, if he lays his whole heart on his business and makes a god of it and thinks more of it than anything else, then the world has come in. It may be very legitimate in its place. It is like fire, which, in its place, is one of the best friends of man; out of place, it is one of the worst enemies of man. Or, it is like water, which we cannot live without, and yet, when not in its place, becomes an enemy.

So my friends, that is the question for you and me to settle. Now look at yourself. Are you getting the victory? Are you growing more even in your disposition? Are you getting mastery over the world and the flesh?

And bear this in mind: Every temptation you overcome makes you stronger to overcome others, while every temptation that defeats you makes you weaker. You can become weaker and weaker, or you can become stronger and stronger. Sin takes the essence out of your muscles, but virtue makes you stronger. How many men have been overcome by some little thing!

Turn a moment to Song of Songs 2:15: *"Take us the foxes, the little foxes, that spoil the vines: for our vines have tender grapes."* A great many people seem to think the following are little things: getting out of patience; using little deceits; telling white lies (as they call them); sending word by the servant that you are not at home when somebody calls on you—all these are little things. Sometimes you can brace yourself up against a great temptation, and, almost before you know it, you fall before some little thing.

Persecution

A great many men are overcome by a little persecution. Do you know, I don't think we have enough persecution nowadays. Some people say we have persecution that is just as hard to bear as in the Dark Ages. Anyway, I think it would be a good thing if we had a little of the old-fashioned kind just now. It would bring out the strongest characters and make us all healthier.

I have heard men get up in prayer meetings and say they were going to make a few remarks and then keep on until you would think they were going to talk all week. If we had a little persecution, people of that kind wouldn't talk so much.

Charles Spurgeon used to say that some Christians would make good martyrs; they would burn well because they are so dry. If there were a few stakes for burning Christians, I think it would take all the piety out of some men. I admit they haven't got much, but then if they are not willing to suffer a little persecution for Christ, they are not fit to be His disciples. We are told, *"All that will live godly in Christ Jesus shall suffer persecution"* (2 Timothy 3:12). Make up your mind to this: If the world has nothing to say against you, Jesus Christ will have nothing to say for you.

The most glorious triumphs of the church have been won in times of persecution. The early church was persecuted for about three hundred years after the crucifixion, and these were years of growth and progress. But then, as Saint Augustine has said, the cross passed from the scene of public executions to the diadem of Caesars, and the downgrade movement began. When the church has joined hands with the state, it has invariably retrograded in spirituality and effectiveness; but the opposition of the state has only served to purify the church of all impurities. It was persecution that gave Scotland to Presbyterianism. It was persecution that gave this country, the United States, to civil and religious freedom.

How are we to overcome in time of persecution? Hear the words of Christ: *"These things I have spoken unto you, that in me ye might have peace. In the world ye shall have tribulation: but be of good cheer; I have overcome the world"* (John 16:33). Paul could testify that, though persecuted, he was never forsaken. He could testify as well that the Lord stood by him and strengthened him and delivered him out of all his persecution and afflictions.

A great many shrink from the Christian life because they will be sneered at. Sometimes when persecution won't bring a man down, flattery will. Foolish people often come up to a man after he has preached and flatter him. Perhaps they will say to some worker in the church, "You talk a great deal better than so-and-so"; and he becomes proud and begins to strut around as if he were the most important person in the town.

I tell you, we have a wily devil to contend with. If he can't overcome you with opposition, he will try flattery or ambition. If those don't serve his purpose, perhaps some affliction or disappointment will come, and he will overcome in that way. But remember that anyone who has Christ to help him can overcome every foe and overcome them singly or collectively. Let them come. If we have Christ within us, we will overthrow them all. Remember what Christ is able to do. In all the ages, men have stood in greater temptations than you and I will ever have to meet.

Now, there is one more thing on this line: I either have to overcome the world, or the world is going to overcome me. I either have to conquer sin in me—or sin about me—and get it under my feet, or it is going to conquer me. A good many people are satisfied with one or two victories and think that is all. I tell you, my dear friends, we have to do something more than that. It is a battle all the time.

We have this to encourage us: We are assured of victory at the end. We are promised a glorious triumph.

Eight "Overcomes"

Here are the eight "overcomes" of Revelation.

The first is:

> *To him that overcometh will I give to eat of the tree of life, which is in the midst of the paradise of God.*
> (Revelation 2:7)

He will have a right to the tree of life. When Adam fell, he lost that right. God turned him out of Eden so he couldn't eat of the Tree of Life and live in his fallen state forever. Perhaps He just took that tree and transplanted it to the garden above, and through the second Adam we are to have the right to eat of it.

The second "overcome" is this:

> *He that overcometh shall not be hurt of the second death.*
> (Revelation 2:11)

Death has no terrors for him; it cannot touch him. Why? Because Christ tasted death for every man. Hence, he is on resurrection ground. Death may take this body, but that is all. This is only the house I live in. We need have no fear of death if we overcome.

Third, Revelation 2 tells us that,

> *To him that overcometh will I give to eat of the hidden manna, and will give him a white stone, and in the stone a new name written, which no man knoweth saving he that receiveth it.* (Revelation 2:17)

If I overcome, God will feed me with bread the world knows nothing about and give me a new name.

The fourth "overcome" is this:

> *And he that overcometh, and keepeth my works unto the end, to him will I give power over the nations.* (Revelation 2:26)

Think of it! What a thing to have: power over the nations! A man who is able to rule himself is the man whom God can trust with power. Only a man who can govern himself is fit to govern other men. I have an idea that we are down here in training, and that God is just polishing us for some higher service. I don't know where the kingdoms are, but if we are to be kings and priests, we must have kingdoms to reign over.

Fifth, Christ promises in Revelation:

> *He that overcometh, the same shall be clothed in white raiment; and I will not blot out his name out of the book of life, but I will confess his name before my Father, and before his angels.* (Revelation 3:5)

Christ will present us to the Father in white garments, without spot or wrinkle. Every fault and stain will be taken out, and we will be made perfect. He who overcomes will not be a stranger in heaven.

The sixth "overcome" is:

> *Him that overcometh will I make a pillar in the temple of my God, and he shall go no more out: and I will*

write upon him the name of my God, and the name of the city of my God, which is new Jerusalem, which cometh down out of heaven from my God: and I will write upon him my new name. (Revelation 3:12)

Think of it! No more backsliding, no more wanderings over the dark mountains of sin, but forever being with the King. And He says, *"I will write upon him the name of my God."*

He is going to put His name upon us. Isn't it grand? Isn't it worth fighting for? It is said when Muhammad came in sight of Damascus and found that they had all left the city, he said, "If they won't fight for this city, what will they fight for?" If they won't fight here for all this reward, what will they fight for?

Seventh, Revelation promises:

To him that overcometh will I grant to sit with me in my throne, even as I also overcame, and am set down with my Father in his throne.
(Revelation 3:21)

My heart has often melted as I have looked at that: The Lord of Glory coming down and saying, "I will grant to you to sit on My throne, even as I sit on My Father's throne, if you will just overcome." Isn't it worth a struggle? How many will fight for a crown that is going to fade away? Yet we are to be placed above the angels, above the archangels, above the seraphim, above the cherubim, away up, upon the throne with God, and there we will be forever with Him. May God put strength into every one of us to fight the battle of life so that we may sit with Him on His throne.

When Frederick of Germany was dying, his own son would not have been allowed to sit with him on the throne, nor would anyone else have been allowed to sit there with him. Yet we are told that we are joint heirs with Jesus Christ and that we are to sit with Him in glory!

And now, the last I like best of all:

He that overcometh shall inherit all things; and I will be his God, and he shall be my son. (Revelation 21:7)

My dear friends, isn't that a high calling? I used to have my Sunday-school children sing, "I want to be an angel," but I have not done so for years. We will be above angels; we will be sons of God. Just see what a kingdom we will come into; we will inherit all things! Do you ask me how much I am worth? I don't know. The Rothschilds cannot compute their wealth. They don't know how many millions they own. That is my condition—I haven't the slightest idea how much I am worth. God has no poor children. If we overcome, we will inherit all things.

Oh, my dear friends, what an inheritance! Let us then get the victory through Jesus Christ, our Lord and Master.

2

Results of True Repentance

I want to call your attention to what true repentance leads to. I am not addressing the unconverted only, because I am one of those who believe that there is a good deal of repentance to be done by the church before much good will be accomplished in the world. I firmly believe that the low standard of Christian living is keeping a good many in the world and in their sins.

When the ungodly see that Christian people do not repent, you cannot expect them to repent and turn away from their sins. I have repented ten thousand times more since

I knew Christ than ever before, and I think most Christians have some things to repent of.

So now, I want to talk to Christians as well as to the unconverted, to myself as well as to one who has never accepted Christ as his Savior.

There are five things that flow out of true repentance:

1. Conviction
2. Contrition
3. Confession of sins
4. Conversion
5. Confession of Jesus Christ before the world

Conviction

When a man is not deeply convicted of sin, it is a pretty sure sign that he has not truly repented. Experience has taught me that men who have very slight conviction of sin sooner or later lapse back into their old lives. For the last few years, I have been a good deal more anxious for a deep and true work in professing converts than I have for great numbers. If a man professes to be converted without realizing the heinousness of his sins, he is likely to be one of those stony-ground hearers who don't amount to anything. The first breath of opposition, the first wave of persecution or ridicule, will suck them back into the world again.

I believe we are making a woeful mistake in taking so many people into the church who have never been truly convicted of sin. Sin is just as black in a man's heart today as it ever was. I sometimes think it is blacker. For the more light a man has, the greater his responsibility, and therefore, the greater need of deep conviction.

William Dawson once told this story to illustrate how humble the soul must be before it can find peace.

He said that at a revival meeting, a little boy who was used to Methodist ways went home to his mother and said, "Mother, John so-and-so is under conviction and seeking peace, but he will not find it tonight, Mother."

"Why, William?" she said.

"Because he is only down on one knee, Mother, and he will never get peace until he is down on both knees."

Until conviction of sin brings us down on both knees, until we are completely humbled, until we have no hope in ourselves left, we cannot find the Savior.

There are three things that lead to conviction: conscience, the Word of God, and the Holy Spirit. All three are used by God. Long before we had any word, God dealt with men through the conscience. That is what made Adam and Eve hide themselves from the presence of the Lord God among the trees of the garden of Eden. (See Genesis 3:8.) That is what convicted Joseph's brothers when they said,

> *"We are verily guilty concerning our brother, in that we saw the anguish of his soul, when he besought us, and we would not hear;" they said (and remember, over twenty years had passed away since they had sold*

him into captivity), "therefore is this distress come upon us."

(Genesis 42:21)

That is what we must use with our children before they are old enough to understand about the Word and the Spirit of God. This is what accuses or excuses the heathen.

Conscience is a divinely implanted faculty in man, telling him that he ought to do right. Someone has said that it was born when Adam and Eve ate of the forbidden fruit, when their eyes were opened and they knew good and evil. It passes judgment without being invited upon our thoughts, words, and actions, approving or condemning accordingly as it judges them to be right or wrong. A man cannot violate his conscience without being self-condemned.

But conscience is not a safe guide, because very often, it will not tell you a thing is wrong until you have done it. It needs illumination from God because it partakes of our fallen nature. Many a person does things that are wrong without being condemned by conscience. Paul said, *"I verily thought with myself, that I ought to do many things contrary to the name of Jesus of Nazareth"* (Acts 26:9). Conscience itself needs to be educated.

Again, conscience is too often like an alarm clock that awakens and rouses at first. But after a time, the man becomes used to it, and it loses its effect. Conscience can be smothered. I think we make a mistake in not preaching more to the conscience.

Hence, in due time, conscience was superseded by the law of God, which in time was fulfilled in Christ. In this Christian land, where men have Bibles, this is the agency by which God produces conviction. The Old Book tells you what is right and wrong before you commit sin; what you need is to learn and appropriate its teachings under the guidance of the Holy Spirit. Conscience compared with the Bible is as a candle compared with the sun in the heavens.

See how the truth convicted those Jews on the day of Pentecost. Peter, filled with the Holy Spirit, preached that,

God hath made that same Jesus, whom ye have crucified, both Lord and Christ. Now when they heard this, they were pricked in their heart, and said unto Peter and to the rest of the apostles, Men and brethren, what shall we do?   (Acts 2:36–37)

Third, the Holy Spirit convicts. I once heard Dr. A. J. Gordon expound on this passage: *"And when he* [the Comforter] *is come, he will reprove the world of sin, and of righteousness, and of judgment: of sin, because they believe not on me"* (John 16:8–9), as follows:

> Some commentators say there was no real conviction of sin in the world until the Holy Spirit came. I think that foreign missionaries will say that that is not true, that a heathen who never heard of Christ may have a tremendous conviction of sin. For notice that God gave conscience first and gave the Comforter afterward. Conscience bears witness to the law; the Comforter bears witness to Christ. Conscience brings legal conviction;

the Comforter brings evangelical conviction. Conscience brings conviction unto condemnation; the Comforter brings conviction until justification. *"He will reprove the world of sin...because they believe not on me"* (John 16:8–9). That is the sin about which He convinces. It does not say that He convinces men of sin because they have stolen or lied or committed adultery, but that the Holy Spirit is to convince men of sin because they have not believed on Jesus Christ. The coming of Jesus Christ into the world made a sin possible that was not possible before. Light reveals darkness; it takes whiteness to bring conviction concerning blackness. There are a great many people in this world who never knew they were sinful until they saw the face of Jesus Christ in all its purity.

Jesus Christ now stands between us and the law. He has fulfilled the law for us. He has settled all claims of the law, and now whatever claim it had upon us has been transferred to Him, so that it is no longer the sin question, but the Son question, that confronts us. And, therefore, you notice that the first thing Peter did, when he began to preach after the Holy Spirit had been sent down, was speak about Christ: *"Him, being delivered by the determinate counsel and foreknowledge of God, ye have taken, and by wicked hands have crucified and slain"* (Acts 2:23). It doesn't say a word about any other kind of sin. That is the sin that runs all through Peter's teaching, and as he preached, the Holy Spirit came down and convicted them, and they cried out, *"What shall we do* [to be saved]*?"* (Acts 2:37).

Well, but we had no part in crucifying Christ; therefore, what is our sin? It is the same sin in another form. They were convicted of crucifying Christ; we are convicted because we have not believed Christ crucified. They were convicted because they had despised and rejected God's Son. The Holy Spirit convicts us because we have not believed in the despised and rejected

One. It is really the same sin in both cases—sin of unbelief in Christ.

Some of the most powerful meetings I have ever been in were those in which there came a sort of hush over the people, and it seemed as if an unseen power gripped their consciences. I remember a man coming to one meeting, and the moment he entered, he felt that God was there. There came a sense of awe upon him, and that very hour, he was convicted and converted.

Contrition

The next thing is contrition—deep, godly sorrow and humiliation of heart because of sin. If there is not true contrition, a man will turn right back into the old sin. That is the trouble with many Christians. A man may get angry, and if there is not much contrition, the next day he will get angry again. A daughter may say mean, cutting things to her mother. Then her conscience troubles her, and she says, "Mother, I am sorry. Forgive me."

But soon there is another outburst of temper, because the contrition is not deep and real. A husband speaks sharp words to his wife and then, to ease his conscience, goes and buys her a bouquet of flowers. Yet he will not go like a man and say he has done wrong.

What God wants is contrition, and if there is not contrition, there is not full repentance. *"The LORD is nigh unto them that are of a broken heart; and saveth such as be of a contrite spirit"* (Psalm 34:18). *"The sacrifices of God are a broken spirit: a broken and a contrite heart, O God, thou wilt not despise"* (Psalm 51:17).

Many sinners are sorry for their sins, sorry that they cannot continue in sin, but they repent only with hearts that are not broken. I don't think we know how to repent nowadays. We need a John the Baptist, wandering through the land, crying, "Repent! Repent!"

Confession of Sins

If we have true contrition, it will lead us to confess our sins. I believe that nine-tenths of the trouble in our Christian lives comes from failing to do this. We try to hide and cover up our sins; there is very little confession of them. Someone has said, "Unconfessed sin in the soul is like a bullet in the body."

If you have no power, it may be there is some sin that needs to be confessed, something in your life that needs straightening out. There is no amount of psalm-singing, no amount of attending religious meetings, no amount of praying or reading your Bible that is going to cover up anything of that kind. It must be confessed, and if I am too proud to confess, I need expect no mercy from God and no answers to my prayers.

The Bible says, *"He that covereth his sins shall not prosper"* (Proverbs 28:13). He may be a man in the pulpit, a priest behind the altar, a king on the throne; I don't care who he is. Man has been trying it for six thousand years. Adam tried it and failed. Moses tried it when he buried the Egyptian whom he killed, but he failed. *"Be sure your sin will find you out"* (Numbers 32:23). You cannot bury your sin so deep that it will not have a resurrection by and by if it has not been blotted out by the Son of God. What man has failed to do for six thousand years, you and I had better give up trying to do.

There are three ways of confessing sin. All sin is against God and must be confessed to Him. There are some sins I need never confess to anyone on earth. If the sin has been between myself and God, I may confess it alone in my closet; I need not whisper it in the ear of any mortal. *"Father, I have sinned against heaven, and before thee"* (Luke 15:18). *"Against thee, thee only, have I sinned, and done this evil in thy sight"* (Psalm 51:4).

But if I have done some man a wrong, and he knows that I have wronged him, I must confess that sin not only to God but also to that man. If I have too much pride to confess it to him, I need not come to God. I may pray and I may weep, but it will do no good. First confess to that man, and then go to God and see how quickly He will hear you and send peace.

> *Therefore if thou bring thy gift to the altar, and there rememberest that thy brother hath ought against thee; leave there thy gift before the altar, and*

*go thy way; first be reconciled to thy
brother, and then come and offer thy
gift.* (Matthew 5:23–24)

That is the Scripture way.

Then, there is another class of sins that
must be confessed publicly. Suppose I have
been known as a blasphemer, a drunkard, or
a morally corrupt person. If I repent of my
sins, I owe the public a confession. The confession should be as public as the transgression. Many people will say some mean thing
about another in the presence of others, and
then try to patch it up by going to that person
alone. The confession should be made so that
all who heard the transgression can hear it.

We are good at confessing other people's
sins, but if it is true repentance, we will have
as much as we can do to look after our own.
When a man or woman gets a good look into
God's looking glass, he doesn't find fault with
other people; he does as much as he can to
take care of his own sins.

*"If we confess our sins, he is faithful and
just to forgive us our sins, and to cleanse us*

from all unrighteousness" (1 John 1:9). Thank God for the Gospel! Fellow Christian, if there is any sin in your life, make up your mind that you will confess it and be forgiven. Do not have any cloud between you and God. Be able to clearly read your title to the mansion Christ has gone to prepare for you.

Conversion

Confession leads to true conversion, and there is no conversion at all until these three steps have been taken.

Now, the word *conversion* means two things. We say a man is converted when he is born again. But it also has a different meaning in the Bible. Peter said, *"Repent ye therefore, and be converted"* (Acts 3:19). The *Revised Version* reads, *"Repent therefore, and **turn"*** (Acts 3:19 RV, emphasis added). Paul said that he was not disobedient to the heavenly vision, but he began to preach to Jews and Gentiles that they should repent and *turn* to God. Some old theologian has said, "Every man is born with his back to God. Repentance is a change of one's course. It is an about-face."

Sin is a turning away from God. As someone has said, it is aversion to God and conversion to the world; and true repentance means conversion to God and aversion to the world. When there is true contrition, the heart is broken *for* sin; when there is true conversion, the heart is broken *from* sin. We leave the old life. We are translated out of the kingdom of darkness into the kingdom of light. Wonderful, isn't it?

Unless our repentance includes this conversion, it is not worth much. If a man continues in sin, it is proof of an idle profession. It is like pumping away continually at the ship's pumps without stopping the leaks. Solomon said, *"If they pray…and confess thy name, and turn from their sin"* (1 Kings 8:35). Prayer and confession would be of no avail while they continued in sin. Let us heed God's call. Let us forsake the old wicked way. Let us return to the Lord, and He will have mercy upon us. Let us also return to our God, for He will abundantly pardon.

If you have never turned to God, turn now. I have no sympathy with the idea that it takes six months or six weeks or six hours to be converted. It doesn't take you very long to turn around, does it? If you know you are wrong, then turn right about.

Confession of Christ

If you are converted, the next step is to confess it openly. Listen:

> *If thou shalt confess with thy mouth the Lord Jesus, and shalt believe in thine heart that God hath raised him from the dead, thou shalt be saved. For with the heart man believeth unto righteousness; and with the mouth confession is made unto salvation.*
>
> (Romans 10:9–10)

Confession of Christ is the culmination of the work of true repentance. We owe it to the world, to our fellow Christians, and to ourselves. Christ died to redeem us, and should we be ashamed or afraid to confess Him? Religion as an abstraction or as a doctrine has little interest for the world, but what people can say from personal experience always has weight.

I remember some meetings being held in a locality where the tide of belief did not rise very quickly, and bitter and reproachful things were being said about the work. But one day, one of the most prominent men in the place rose and said, "I want it to be known that I am a disciple of Jesus Christ; and if there is any enmity to be cast on His cause, I am prepared to take my share of it."

It went through the meeting like an electric current, and a blessing came at once to his own soul and to the souls of others.

Men come to me and say, "Do you mean to affirm, Mr. Moody, that I have to make a public confession when I accept Christ; do you mean to say I have to confess Him in my place of business, and in my family? Am I to let the whole world know that I am on His side?"

That is precisely what I mean. A great many are willing to accept Christ, but they are not willing to publish it, to confess it. A great many are looking at the lions and the bears in the way.

RESULTS OF TRUE REPENTANCE

Now, my friends, the devil's mountains are only made of smoke. He can throw a straw into your path and make a mountain of it. He says to you, "You cannot confess and pray to your family; why, you'll break down! You cannot tell it to your colleague; he will laugh at you." But when you accept Christ, you will have power to confess Him.

There was a young man in the West who had been more or less interested about his soul's salvation. One afternoon, in his office, he said, "I will accept Jesus Christ as my Lord and Savior."

He went home and told his wife (who nominally professed religion) that he had made up his mind to serve Christ, and he added, "After supper tonight I am going to take the company into the drawing room and erect the family altar."

"Well," said his wife, "you know some of the gentlemen who are coming to tea are skeptics, and they are older than you are, and don't you think you had better wait until after they have gone or else go out in the kitchen and have your first prayer with the servants?"

The young man thought for a few moments, and then he said, "I have asked Jesus Christ into my house for the first time, and I will take Him into the best room, not into the kitchen."

So he called his friends into the drawing room. There was some sneering, but he read and prayed. That man later became Chief Justice of the United States Court. Never be ashamed of the Gospel of Christ, for it is the power of God unto salvation. (See Romans 1:6.)

A young man enlisted in the army and was sent to his regiment. The first night, he was in the barracks with about fifteen other young men who passed the time playing cards and gambling. Before retiring, he fell on his knees and prayed, and they began to curse him and jeer at him and throw boots at him.

So it went on the next night and the next, and finally the young man went and told the chaplain what had taken place and asked what he should do.

"Well," said the chaplain, "you are not at home now, and the other men have just as much right in the barracks as you have. It makes them mad to hear you pray, and the Lord will hear you just as well if you say your prayers in bed and don't provoke them."

For weeks after their meeting, the chaplain did not see the young man, but one day he met him and asked, "By the way, did you take my advice?"

"I did, for two or three nights."

"How did it work?"

"Well," said the young man, "I felt like a whipped hound, and the third night I got out of bed, knelt down, and prayed."

"How did that work?" asked the chaplain.

The young soldier answered, "We have a prayer meeting there now every night. Three have been converted, and we are praying for the rest."

Friends, I am so tired of weak Christianity. Let us be out and out for Christ; let us give no uncertain sound. If the world wants to call us fools, let them do it. It is only a little while; the crowning day is coming. Thank God for the privilege we have of confessing Christ.

❧ 3 ❧

Let Your Light Shine

*"They that be wise shall shine as the brightness
of the firmament; and they that turn many to
righteousness as the stars for ever and ever."*
—Daniel 12:3

That is the testimony of an old man and one who had the richest and deepest experience of any man living on the face of the earth at the time. He was taken down to Babylon when he was a young man; some Bible students think he was not more than twenty years of age. If anyone had said, when this young Hebrew was carried away into captivity, that he would outrank all the mighty men of that day—that all the generals who had been victorious in almost every nation at that time were to be eclipsed by this young slave—probably no one would have believed it. Yet for five hundred years, no man whose life is recorded in history shone as did this man. He outshone Nebuchadnezzar, Belshazzar, Cyrus, Darius, and all the princes and mighty monarchs of his day.

We are not told when he was converted to a knowledge of the true God, but I think we have good reason to believe that he had been brought under the influence of Jeremiah the prophet. Evidently some earnest, godly man, and no worldly man who only professed religion, had made a deep impression on him. Someone had, at any rate, taught him how he was to serve God.

We hear people nowadays talking about the hardness of the field where they labor; they say their position is a very special one. Think of the field in which Daniel had to work. He was not only a slave, but he was held captive by a nation that detested the Hebrews. The language was unknown to him. There he was among idolaters, yet he commenced at once to shine. He took his stand for God from the very first, and so he went on through his whole life. He gave the dew of his youth to God, and he continued to be faithful until his pilgrimage was ended.

Notice that all those who have made a deep impression on the world and have shone most brightly have been men who lived in a dark day. Look at Joseph. He was sold as a slave into Egypt by the Ishmaelites, yet he took his God with him into captivity, as Daniel later did. And he remained true to the last; he did not give up his faith because he had been taken away from home and placed among idolaters. He stood firm, and God stood by him.Look at Moses, who turned his back upon the gilded palaces of Egypt and identified himself with his despised and downtrodden nation. If a man ever had a hard field, it was Moses; yet he shone brightly and was faithful to his God.

Elijah lived in a far darker day than we do. The whole nation was going over to idolatry. Ahab and his queen and the entire royal court were throwing their influence against the worship of the true God. Yet Elijah stood firm and shone brightly in that dark and evil day. How his name stands out on the page of history!

Look at John the Baptist. I used to think I would like to live in the days of the prophets, but I have given up that idea. You may be sure that when a prophet appears on the scene, everything is dark, and the professing church of God has gone over to the service of the god of this world. So it was when John the Baptist made his appearance. See how his name shines out today! Eighteen centuries have rolled away, and yet the fame of that wilderness preacher shines brighter than ever. He was looked down upon in his day and generation, but he has outlived all his enemies. His name will be revered and his work remembered as long as the church is on the earth.

Talk about your field being a hard one! See how Paul shone for God as he went out, the first missionary to the heathen, telling them of the God whom he served and who had sent His Son to die a cruel death in order to save the world. Men reviled him and his teachings; they scorned him by laughing when he spoke of the crucified One. But he went on preaching the Gospel of the Son of God. He was regarded as a poor tentmaker by the great and mighty ones of his day. However, no one can now tell the name of any of his persecutors or of those who lived at that time unless their names happen to be associated with his.

Now, the fact is, all men like to shine. We may as well acknowledge it at once. Go into business circles, and see how men struggle to get into the front rank. Everyone wants to outshine his neighbor and to stand at the head of his profession. Go into the political world, and see how there is a struggle going on as to who will be the greatest. If you go into a school, you find that there is a rivalry among the boys and girls; they all want to stand at the top of the class. When a boy or girl does reach this position and outranks all the rest, his or her mother is very proud of her child. She will manage to tell all the neighbors how her child has done well and what a number of prizes the child has gained. Go into the army and you find the same thing—one trying to outstrip the other. Everyone is very anxious to shine and rise above his comrades. Go among the young men in their games, and see how anxious the one is to outdo the other. So we all have that desire in us; we like to shine above our fellows.

And yet there are very few who can really shine in the world. Once in a while, one man will outstrip all his competitors. Every four years, a struggle goes on throughout our country to determine who will be the President of the United States, the battle raging for six months or a year. Yet only one man can get the prize. There are a good many struggling to get the place, but many are disappointed because only one can attain the coveted prize. But in the kingdom of God, the very least and the very weakest may shine if they will. Not only can one obtain the prize, but all may have it, if they so desire it.

It does not say in the passage from Daniel that the statesmen are going to shine as the brightest of the firmament. The statesmen of Babylon are gone; their very names are forgotten.

It does not say that the nobility are going to shine. Earth's nobility are soon forgotten. John Bunyan, the Bedford tinker, has outlived the whole crowd of those who were the nobility in his day. They lived for self, and their memory is blotted out. He lived for God and for souls, and his name is as fragrant as it ever was.

We are not told that the merchants are going to shine. Who can tell the name of any of the millionaires of Daniel's day? They were all buried in oblivion a few years after their death. Who were the mighty conquerors of that day? Few can tell. It is true that we hear of Nebuchadnezzar, but probably we would not have known very much about him except for his relations to the prophet Daniel.

How different it is with this faithful prophet of the Lord! Twenty-five centuries have passed away, and his name shines on and on and on, brighter and brighter. And it is going to shine while the church of God exists. *"They that be wise shall shine as the brightness of the firmament; and they that turn many to righteousness as the stars for ever and ever"* (Daniel 12:3).

How quickly the glory of this world fades away! Not a very long time ago the great Napoleon almost made the earth tremble. How he blazed and shone as an earthly warrior for a little while! A few years passed, and a little island held that once proud and mighty conqueror. He died a poor, broken-hearted prisoner. Where is he today? Who in all the world will say that Napoleon lives in his heart's affections?

But look at this despised and hated Hebrew prophet. They wanted to put him into the lions' den because he was too sanctimonious and too religious. Yet see how green his memory is today! How his name is loved and honored for his faithfulness to his God.

Many years ago, I was in Paris at the time of the Great Exhibition. Napoleon III was then in his glory. Cheer after cheer would rise as he drove along the streets of the city.

A few short years and he fell from his lofty estate. He died in exile from his country and his throne, and where is his name today? Very few think about him at all, and if his name is mentioned, it is not with love and esteem.

How empty and short-lived are the glory and the pride of this world! If we are wise, we will live for God and eternity; we will get outside of ourselves and will care nothing for the honor and glory of this world. In Proverbs 11:30, we read, *"He that winneth souls is wise."* If any man by a godly life and example can win one soul to God, his life will not have been a failure. He will have outshone all the mighty men of his day because he will have set a stream in motion that will flow on and on for ever and ever.

God has left us down here to shine. We are not here to buy and sell and get gain, to accumulate wealth, or to acquire worldly position. If we are Christians, this earth is not our home; our home is up yonder. God has sent us into the world to shine for Him—to light up this dark world. Christ came to be the Light of the World, but men put out that light.

In the Gospel of Matthew, before Christ went up on high, He said to His disciples, *"Ye are the light of the world"* (Matthew 5:14). He also told them, *"Go ye therefore, and teach all nations, baptizing them in the name of the Father, and of the Son, and of the Holy Ghost"* (Matthew 28:19).

So God has called us to shine, just as much as Daniel was sent into Babylon to shine. Let no man or woman say that he or she cannot shine because he or she does not have as much influence as some others may have. What God wants you to do is use the influence you have. Daniel probably did not have much influence down in Babylon at first, but God soon gave him more because he was faithful and used what he had.

Remember, a small light will do a good deal when it is in a very dark place. Put one little candle in the middle of a large hall, and it will give a good deal of light.

Out in the prairie regions, when meetings were held at night in log schoolhouses, the announcement of the meeting was given out in this way: "A meeting will be held by early candlelight."

The first man who came brought a tallow candle with him. It was perhaps all he had, but he brought it and set it on the desk. It did not light the building much, but it was better than nothing at all. The next man brought his candle, and the next family brought theirs. By the time the house was full, there was plenty of light. So if we all shine a little, there will be a good deal of light. That is what God wants us to do. If we cannot all be lighthouses, any one of us can at any rate be a tallow candle.

A little light will sometimes do a great deal. The city of Chicago was set on fire by a cow kicking over a lamp, and a hundred thousand people were burned out of house and home. Do not let Satan take advantage of you and make you think that because you cannot do a great thing, you cannot do anything at all.

Then, we must remember that we are to let our light shine. Matthew 5:16 does not say, "*Make* your light shine." It says, *"Let your light so shine"* (emphasis added). You do not have *make* your light to shine; all you have to do is *let* it shine.

I remember hearing of a man at sea who was very seasick. If there is a time when a man feels that he cannot do any work for the Lord, it is then, in my opinion. While this man was sick, he heard that someone had fallen overboard. He was wondering if he could do anything to help save the man. He found a light and held it up to the porthole. The drowning man was saved. When this man got over his attack of sickness, he went on deck one day and talked with the man who was rescued.

The saved man gave this testimony. He said he had gone down the second time and was just going down again for the last time when he put out his hand. Just then, he said, someone held a light at the porthole, and the light fell on his hand. A sailor caught him by the hand and pulled him into the lifeboat.

It seemed a small thing to do to hold up the light, yet it saved the man's life. If you cannot do some great thing, you can hold the light for some poor, perishing drunkard who may be won to Christ and delivered from destruction. Let us take the torch of salvation and go into the dark homes and hold up Christ to people as the Savior of the world. If the perishing masses are to be reached, we must lay our lives right alongside theirs and pray with them and labor for them.

It wouldn't say much for a man's Christianity if he is saved himself and is not willing to try to save others. It seems to me the basest ingratitude if we do not reach out a hand to others who are down in the same pit from which we were delivered. Who is able to reach and help drinking men as well as those who have themselves been slaves to the intoxicating cup? Will you not go out this very day and seek to rescue these men? If we were all to do what we can, we would soon empty the drinking saloons.

I remember reading about a blind man who was found sitting at the corner of a street in a great city with a lantern beside him. Someone went up to him and asked what he had the lantern there for, seeing that he was blind and the light was the same to him as the darkness. The blind man replied, "I have it so that no one may stumble over me."

Dear friends, let us think of that. Where one man reads the Bible, one hundred people read you and me. That is what Paul meant when he said we were to be living epistles of Christ, known and read by all men.

I don't think much will be accomplished by sermons if we do not preach Christ in our lives, as well. If we do not commend the Gospel to people by our holy walk and conversation, we will not win them to Christ. Some little act of kindness will perhaps do more to influence them than any number of long sermons.

A vessel trying to make for the harbor of Cleveland was caught in a storm on Lake Erie. At the entrance of that port, they had what are called the upper lights and the lower lights.

Back on the bluffs were the upper lights, burning brightly enough, but when they came near the harbor, they could not see the lights showing the entrance to it. The pilot said he thought they had better get back on the lake again. The captain said he was sure they would go down if they went back, and he urged the pilot to do what he could to gain the harbor. The pilot said there was very little hope of making the harbor because he had nothing to guide him as to how he should steer his ship. They tried all they could to get her in. She rode on the top of the waves and then into the trough of the sea, and at last they found themselves stranded on the beach, where the vessel was dashed to pieces. Someone had neglected the lower lights, and they had gone out.

Let us take warning. God keeps the upper lights burning as brightly as ever, but He has left us down here to keep the lower lights burning. We are to represent Him here, as Christ represents us up yonder. I sometimes think if we had as poor a representative in the courts above as God has down here on earth, we would have a pretty poor chance of going to heaven. Let us be ready and have our lights burning brightly so that others may see the way and not walk in darkness.

Speaking of a lighthouse reminds me of what I heard about a man in Minnesota who, some years ago, was caught in a fearful storm. That state is cursed with storms that come sweeping down so suddenly in the wintertime that escape is difficult. The snow will fall and the wind will beat into the face of the traveler so that he cannot see two feet ahead. Many men have been lost on the prairies when caught in one of these storms.

This man was caught and was almost on the point of giving up when he saw a little light in a log house. He managed to get there and found a shelter from the fury of the tempest. He is now a wealthy man. As soon as he was able, he bought the farm and built a beautiful house on the spot where the log building stood. On the top of a tower, he put a revolving light, and every night when a storm comes, he lights it up in the hope that it may be the means of saving someone else.

That is true gratitude, and that is what God wants us to do. If He has rescued us and brought us up out of the horrible pit, let us be always looking to see if there is someone else whom we can help to save.

I remember hearing of two men who were in charge of a revolving light in a lighthouse on a stormy, rockbound coast. Somehow the machinery went wrong, and the light did not revolve. They were so afraid that those at sea would mistake it for some other light that they worked the entire night through to keep the light moving around. Let us keep our lights in the proper place so that the world may see that the religion of Christ is not a sham but a reality. It is said that in the Greek Olympics they had one game where the men ran with lights. They lit a torch at the altar and ran a certain distance; sometimes they were on horseback. If a man came in with his light still burning, he received a prize; if his light had gone out, he lost the prize.

How many there are who, in their old age, have lost their light and their joy! They were once burning and shining lights in the family, in the Sunday school, and in the church. But something has come between them and

God—the world or self—and their lights have gone out.

Reader, if you are one who has had this experience, may God help you to come back to the altar of the Savior's love and light up your torch anew so that you can go out into the lanes and alleys and let the light of the Gospel shine in these dark homes.

As I have already said, if we only lead one soul to Jesus Christ, we may set a stream in motion that will flow on, even when we are dead and gone. Up on the mountainside there is a little spring; it seems so small that an ox might drink it up in one gulp. By and by it becomes a rivulet; other rivulets run into it. Before long, it is a large brook, and then it becomes a broad river sweeping onward to the sea. On its banks are cities, towns, and villages where many thousands live. Vegetation flourishes on every side, and commerce is carried down its stately bosom to distant lands.

So if you turn one to Christ, that one may turn a hundred. Those hundred may turn a thousand, and so the stream, small at first, goes on broadening and deepening as it rolls toward eternity.

In the book of Revelation, we read,

> *I heard a voice from heaven saying unto me, Write, Blessed are the dead which die in the Lord from hence-forth: Yea, saith the Spirit, that they may rest from their labours; and their works do follow them.*
>
> (Revelation 14:13)

There are many of whom we read in the Scriptures who lived so many years and then they died. The cradle and the grave are brought close together; they lived and they died, and that is all we know about them. So in these days, you could write on the tombstone of a great many professing Christians that they were born on such a day and they died on such a day; there is nothing whatever between.

But there is one thing you cannot bury with a good man: his influence still lives. They have not buried Daniel yet; his influence is as great today as it ever was. Do you tell me that Joseph is dead? His influence still lives and will continue to live on and on. You may bury the frail tenement of clay that a good man lives in, but you cannot get rid of his influence and example. Paul was never more powerful than he is today.

Do you tell me that John Howard, who went into so many of the dark prisons in Europe, is dead? Is Henry Martyn or William Wilberforce or John Bunyan dead? At one time, people could go into the South and there find millions of men and women who once were slaves. If the name of Wilberforce were mentioned to any of these former slaves, how quickly their eyes would light up. He lived for something else besides himself, and his memory will never die out of the hearts of those for whom he lived and labored.

Is John Wesley or George Whitefield dead? The names of those great evangelists were never more honored than they are now. Is John Knox dead? You can go to any part of Scotland and feel the power of his influence.

I will tell you the people who are dead. The enemies of these servants of God, those who persecuted them and told lies about them. But the men themselves have outlived all the lies that were uttered concerning them. Not only that, they will shine in another world. How true are the words of Daniel 12:3: *"They that be wise shall shine as the brightness of the firmament; and they that turn many to righteousness as the stars for ever and ever."*

Let us go on turning as many as we can to righteousness. Let us be dead to the world, to its lies, its pleasures, and its ambitions. Let us live for God, continually going forth to win souls for Him.

Let me quote a few words by Dr. Thomas Chalmers:

> Thousands of men breathe, move and live, pass off the stage of life, and are heard no more—Why? They do not partake of good in the world, and none were blessed by them. None could point to them as the means of their redemption. Not a line they wrote, not a word they spoke could be recalled, and so they perished. Their light went out in darkness, and they were not remembered more

than insects of yesterday. Will you thus live and die, O man immortal?

Live for something. Do good, and leave behind you a monument of virtue that the storms of time can never destroy. Write your name in kindness, love, and mercy on the hearts of the thousands you come in contact with year by year; you will never be forgotten. No, your name, your deeds will be as legible on the hearts you leave behind as the stars on the brow of evening. Good deeds will shine as the stars of heaven.

❧4❧

"Come Thou and All Thy House into the Ark"

I want to call your attention to a text that you will find in Genesis 7:1. When God speaks, you and I can afford to listen. It is not man speaking now, but it is God: *"The LORD said unto Noah, Come thou and all thy house into the ark."*

Perhaps some skeptic is reading this, and perhaps some church member will join with him and say, "I hope Mr. Moody is not going to talk about the ark. I thought that was given up by all intelligent people."

But I want to say that I haven't given it up. When I do, I am going to give up the whole

Bible. There is hardly any portion of the Old Testament Scripture that the Son of God did not set His seal to when He was down here in the world.

Men say, "I don't believe in the story of the flood." Christ connected His own return to this world with that flood:

> *And as it was in the days of Noe [Noah], so shall it be also in the days of the Son of man. They did eat, they drank, they married wives, they were given in marriage, until the day that Noe entered into the ark, and the flood came, and destroyed them all.*
> (Luke 17:26–27)

I believe the story of the flood just as much as I do the third chapter of John. I pity any man who is picking the Old Book to pieces. The moment that we give up any one of these things, we touch the deity of the Son of God. I have noticed that when a man does begin to pick the Bible to pieces, it doesn't take him long to tear it all to pieces. What is the use of working for five years on what you can do in five minutes?

A Solemn Message

One hundred and twenty years before God spoke the words of the text from Genesis, Noah had received the most awful communication that ever came from heaven to earth. No man up to that time, and I think no man since, had ever received such a communication. God said that because of the wickedness of the world, He was going to destroy the world by water. We can have no idea of the extent and character of that ancient wickedness. The Bible piles one expression on another in its effort to emphasize it.

> *God saw that the wickedness of man was great in the earth, and that every imagination of the thoughts of his heart was only evil continually. And it repented the LORD that he had made man on the earth, and it grieved him at his heart….The earth also was corrupt before God, and the earth was filled with violence. And God looked upon the earth, and, behold, it was corrupt; for all flesh had corrupted his way upon the earth.* (Genesis 6:5–6, 11–12)

Men lived five hundred years and more then, and so had time to mature in their sins.

How the Message Was Received

For one hundred and twenty years, God contended with those ancient sinners. He never smites without warning, and they had their warning. Every time Noah drove a nail into the ark, it was a warning to them. Every sound of the hammer echoed, "I believe in God." If they had repented and cried as the people at Nineveh did, I believe God would have heard their cry and spared them. But there was no cry for mercy. I have no doubt that they ridiculed the idea that God was going to destroy the world. I have no doubt that there were atheists who said there was no God anyway

I talked to an atheist some time ago. I said, "How do you account for the formation of the world?"

"Oh! Force and matter work together, and by chance the world was created."

I responded to him, "It is an amazing thing that your tongue isn't on top of your head if force and matter just threw it together in that matter. If I would take out my watch and say that force and matter worked together and out came the watch, you would say I was a lunatic of the first order, wouldn't you? And yet they say that this old world was made by chance! 'It threw itself together'!"

I met a man in Scotland who held the view that there was no God. I asked him, "How do you account for creation, for all these rocks?" (They have a great many rocks in Scotland.)

"Why," he said, "any schoolboy could account for that."

"Well, how was the first rock made?"

"Out of sand."

"How was the first sand made?"

"Out of rock."

You see, he had it all arranged so nicely. Sand and rock, rock and sand. I have no doubt that Noah had these men to contend with.

Then, there was a class called agnostics, and there are a good many of their grandchildren alive today. There was another class who said they believed there was a God. They couldn't make themselves believe that the world happened by chance, but they believed that God was too merciful to punish sin. He was so full of compassion and love that He couldn't punish sin. The drunkard, the harlot, the gambler, the murderer, the thief, and the libertine would all share alike with the saints at the end. Suppose the governor of your state was so tenderhearted that he could not bear to have a man suffer, could not bear to see a man put in jail, and he would go and set all the prisoners free. How long would he be governor? You would have him out of office before the sun set. These very men who talk about God's mercy would be the first to raise a cry against a governor who would not have a man put in prison when he had done wrong.

Another class took the ground that God could not completely destroy the world. They might have a great flood that would rise up to the meadowlands and lowlands, but all they would need to do is go up on the hills and mountains. That would be a hundred times better than Noah's ark. Or they could build rafts, which would be a good deal better than that ark. They had never seen such an ugly looking thing. It was about five hundred feet long and about eighty feet wide and fifty feet high. It had three stories and only one small window.

And then, I suppose there was a large class who held the opinion that Noah must be wrong because he was in the minority. That is a great argument now, you know. Noah was greatly in the minority. But he went on working.

I don't doubt that they had saloons back then, because we read that *"the earth was filled with violence"* (Genesis 6:11), and wherever you have alcohol, you have violence. We read also that Noah planted a vineyard and fell into the sin of intemperance. He was a righteous man, and if he did that, what must the others have done? Well, if they had saloons, no doubt they sang ribald songs about Noah and his ark. If they had theaters, they likely acted it out, and mothers took their children to see it.

And if they had the press in those days, every now and then there would appear an editorial about "Noah and his folly." Reporters would come and interview him, and if they had an Associated Press, every few days a dispatch would be sent telling how the work on the ark was progressing. And perhaps they had excursions and offered as an inducement that people could go through the ark. And if Noah happened to be around, they would nudge each other and say, "That's Noah. Don't you think there is a strange look in his eye?"

As a Scotsman would say, they thought him a little daft. Thank God a man can afford to be mad. A mad man thinks everyone else mad but himself. A drunkard does not call himself mad when he is drinking up all his means. Those men who stand and deal out death and damnation to men are not called "mad," but a man is called "mad" when he gets into the ark and is saved for time and eternity. And I expect if the word *crank* was in use, they called Noah "an old crank."

And so, all manner of sport was made of Noah and his ark. The businessmen went on buying and selling, while Noah went on preaching and toiling. They perhaps had some astronomers who were gazing up at the stars and saying, "Don't you be concerned. There is no sign of a coming storm in the heavens. We are very wise men, and if there was a storm coming, we would read it in the heavens." And they had geologists digging away, and they said, "There is no sign in the earth." Even the carpenters who helped build the ark might have made fun of him, but they were like lots of people at the present time who will help build a church, perhaps even give money for its support, but never enter it themselves.

Well, things went on as usual. Little lambs skipped on the hillsides each spring. Men sought after wealth, and if they had leases, I expect they ran for longer periods than ours do. We think ninety-nine years is a long time, but I don't doubt that theirs ran for 999 years. And when they came to sign a lease, they would say with a twinkle in their eyes, "Why, this old Noah says the world is coming to an end in one hundred and twenty years, and it's been twenty years since he started the story. But I guess I will sign the lease and risk it."

Someone has said that Noah must have been deaf, or he could not have otherwise stood the jeers and sneers of his countrymen. But if he was deaf to the voice of men, he certainly heard the voice of God when He told him to build the ark.

I can imagine one hundred years have rolled away, and the work on the ark has ceased. Men say, "What has he stopped work for?" He has gone on a preaching tour to tell the people of the coming storm, to tell them that God is going to sweep every man from the face of the earth unless he is in the ark. But he cannot get anyone to believe him except his own family. Some of the old men have passed away, and they died saying, "Noah is wrong!"

Poor Noah! He must have had a hard time of it. I don't think I would have had the grace to work one hundred and twenty years without a convert. But he just toiled on, believing the word of God.

And at some point, the one hundred and twenty years were up. In the spring of the year, Noah did not plant anything because he knew the flood was coming, and the people said, "Every year before he has planted, but this year he thinks the world is going to be destroyed, and he hasn't planted anything."

Moving In

I can imagine one beautiful morning, not a cloud to be seen; Noah has gotten his communication. He has heard the voice that he heard one hundred and twenty years before—the same old voice. Perhaps there had been silence for one hundred and twenty years. But the voice rang through his soul once again: *"Noah, Come thou and all thy house into the ark"* (Genesis 7:1). The word *come* occurs about nineteen hundred times in the Bible, it is said, and this is the first time. It meant salvation. You can see Noah and his entire family moving into the ark. They are loading their household furniture.

Some of Noah's neighbors might have said, "Noah, what is your hurry? You will have plenty of time to get into that old ark. What is your hurry? There are no windows, and you cannot look out to see when the storm is coming." But he heard the voice and obeyed.

Some of his relatives might have said, "What are you going to do with the old homestead?"

Noah told them, "I don't want it. The storm is coming." He told them that the day of grace was coming to an end, that worldly wealth was of no value, and that the ark was the only place of safety. We must bear in mind that these railroads that we think so much of will soon go down; they only run for time, not for eternity. The heavens will be on fire, and then what will property, honor, and position in society be worth?

The first thing that alarmed Noah's neighbors was rising one morning, and behold—the heavens were filled with the fowls of the air. They were flying into the ark, two by two. They came from the deserts and the mountains; they came from all parts of the world. They were going into the ark. It must have been a strange sight. I can hear the people cry,

"Great God! What is the meaning of this?" And they looked down on the earth, and, with great alarm and surprise, they saw little insects creeping up two by two, coming from all parts of the world. Then behold! Cattle and beasts came, two by two. The neighbors cried out, "What does this mean?"

They ran to their statesmen and wise men who had told them there was no sign of a coming storm, and they asked them why it was that those birds, animals, and creeping things were going toward the ark as if guided by some unseen hand.

"Well," the statesmen and wise men said, "We cannot explain it; but give yourselves no trouble; God is not going to destroy the world. Business was never better than it is now. Do you think if God was going to destroy the world, He would let us go on as prosperously as He has? There is no sign of a coming storm. What has made these creeping insects and these wild beasts of the forest go into the ark, we do not know. We cannot understand it; it is very strange. But there is no sign that anything is going to happen. The stars are bright, and the sun shines as clear as it ever did. Everything moves on as it has been moving for all time past. You can hear the children playing in the street. You can hear the voice of the bride and bridegroom in the land, and all is merry as ever."

I imagine the alarm passed away, and they fell into their regular courses. Noah came out and said, "The door is going to be shut. Come in. God is going to destroy the world. See the animals, how they have come up. The communication has come to them directly from heaven." But the people only continued to mock him.

Do you know, when the one hundred and twenty years were up, God gave the world seven days of grace? Did you ever notice that? If there had been a cry during those seven days, I believe it would have been heard. But there was none.

At length, the last day had come, the last hour, the last minute, the last second. God Almighty came down and shut the door of that ark. No angel, no man, but God Himself shut the door, and once the Master has risen and shut the door, the doom of the world is sealed. The doom of that old world was forever sealed. The sun had gone down upon the glory of that old world for the last time. You could hear the mutterings of the storm off in the distance. You could hear the thunder rolling. The lightning began to flash, and the old world reeled. The storm burst upon them, and that old ark of Noah's would have been worth more than the whole world to them.

I want to say to any scoffer who reads this that you can laugh at the Bible, scoff at your mother's God, or laugh at ministers and Christians, but the hour is coming when one promise in that Old Book will be worth more to you than ten thousand worlds like this.

The windows of heaven were opened and the fountains of the great deep were broken up. The waters came bubbling up, and the sea burst its bounds and leaped over its walls. The rivers began to swell.

The people living in the lowlands fled to the mountains and highlands. They fled up the hillsides. And there was a wail going up: "Noah! Noah! Noah! Let us in."

They left their homes and came to the ark. They pounded on the ark. Hear their cry: "Noah! Let us in. Noah! Have mercy on us."

"I am your nephew."

"I am your niece."

"I am your uncle."

Ah, there is a voice inside, saying, "I would like to let you in, but God has shut the door, and I cannot open it!"

God shut that door! When the door is shut, there is no hope. Their cry for mercy was too late; their day of grace was closed. Their last hour had come. God had pleaded with them. God had invited them to come in, but they had mocked at the invitation. They scoffed and ridiculed the idea of a deluge. Now it was too late.

God did not permit anyone to survive to tell us how they perished. When Job lost his family, there came a messenger to him, but no messenger from these ancient sinners came. Not even Noah himself could see the world perish. If he could, he would have seen men and women and children dashing against that ark and the waves rising higher and higher while those outside were perishing, dying in unbelief.

Some thought to escape by climbing the trees and thought the storm would soon go down, but it rained on, day and night for forty days and forty nights. They were swept away as the waves dashed against them. The statesmen and astronomers and great men called for mercy, but it was too late.

They had disobeyed the God of mercy. He had called, and they had refused. He had pleaded with them, but they had laughed and mocked. But now the time had come for judgment instead of mercy.

Judgment

The time is coming again when God will deal in judgment with the world. It is but a little while. We know not when, but it is sure to come. God's Word has gone forth that this world will be rolled together like a scroll and will be on fire. What then will become of your soul? It is a loving call: *"Come thou and all thy house into the ark"* (Genesis 7:1).

Twenty-four hours before the rain began to fall, Noah's ark, if it had been sold at auction, would not have brought as much as it would be worth for kindling. But twenty-four hours after the rain began to fall, Noah's ark was worth more than the entire world. There was not, then, a man living who would not have given all he was worth for a seat in the ark.

You may turn away and laugh. "I believe in Christ," you say. "I would rather be without Him than have Him, though."

But bear in mind, the time is coming when Christ will be worth more to you than ten thousand worlds like this. Bear in mind that He is offered to you now. This is a day of grace; it is a day of mercy. You will find, if you read your Bible carefully, that God always precedes judgment with grace. Grace is a forerunner of judgment. He called these men in the days of Noah in love. They would have been saved if they had repented in those one hundred and twenty years. When Christ came to plead with the people in Jerusalem, it was their day of grace, but they mocked and laughed at Him. He said,

> *O Jerusalem, Jerusalem, thou that killest the prophets, and stonest them which are sent unto thee, how often would I have gathered thy children together, even as a hen gathereth her chickens under her wings, and ye would not!* (Matthew 23:37)

Forty years afterward, thousands of the people begged that their lives might be spared and eleven hundred thousand perished in that city.

In 1857, a revival swept over this country in the east and onto the western cities, clear over to the Pacific coast. It was God calling the nation to Himself. Half a million people united with the church at that time. Then, the Civil War broke out. We were baptized with the Holy Spirit in 1857, and we were baptized in blood in 1861. It was a call of mercy preceding judgment.

Are Your Children Safe?

The text that I have selected, Genesis 7:1, has a special application to Christian people and to parents. This command of Scripture was given to Noah, not only for his own safety but also for that of his household, and the question that I put to each father and mother is this: Are your children in the ark of God? You may scoff at it, but it is a very important question. Are all your children in? Are all your grandchildren in? Do not rest day or night until you get your children in.

I believe my children have fifty temptations where I had one. I am one of those who believe that in the great cities, there is a snare set upon the corner of every street for our sons and daughters, and I don't believe it is our business to spend our time in accumulating stocks and bonds. Have I done all that I can to get my children in? That is the question we need to ask.

Now, let me ask another question: What would Noah's feelings have been if, when God called him into the ark, his children would not have gone with him? If he had lived such a false life that his children had no faith in his word, what would his feelings have been? He would have said, "There is my poor boy on the mountain. Would to God that I had died in his place! I would rather have perished than had him perish." David cried over his son, *"O my son Absalom, my son, my son Absalom! would God I had died for thee, O Absalom, my son, my son!"* (2 Samuel 18:33). Noah loved his children, and they had confidence in him.

Someone sent me a paper a number of years ago containing an article that was marked. Its title was "Are All the Children In?" An old wife lay dying. She was nearly one hundred years of age, and the husband who had taken the journey with her sat by her side. She was just breathing faintly, but suddenly she revived, opened her eyes, and said, "Why! It is dark."

"Yes, Janet, it is dark," her husband replied.

"Is it night?"

"Oh, yes! It is midnight."

"Are all the children in?"

There was that old mother living life over again. Her youngest child had been in the grave twenty years, but she was traveling back into the old days. She fell asleep in Christ, asking, "Are all the children in?"

Dear friend, are they all in? Put the question to yourself now. Is John in? Is James in? Or is he immersed in business and pleasure? Is he living a double and dishonest life? Say, where is your boy, mother? Where is your son, your daughter? Is it well with your children? Can you say it is?

After being superintendent of a Sunday school in Chicago for a number of years, I used to think that if I would ever stand before an audience I would speak to no one but parents; that would be my chief business. At this school of more than a thousand members, children came from godless homes, and their mothers and fathers worked against me, taking the children off on excursions on Sundays and doing all they could to break up the work I was trying to do.

It is an old saying, "Get the lamb, and you will get the sheep." I gave that up years ago. Give me the sheep, and then I will have someone to nurse the lamb. But get a lamb and convert him, and if he has a godless father and mother, you will have little chance with that child. What we lack are godly homes. The home was established long before the church.

I have no sympathy with the idea that our children have to grow up before they are converted. Once, I saw a lady with three daughters at her side, and I stepped up to her and asked her if she was a Christian.

"Yes, sir."

Then I asked the oldest daughter if she was a Christian. Her chin began to quiver, tears came into her eyes, and she said, "I wish I was." The mother looked very angrily at me and said, "I don't want you to speak to my children on that subject. They don't understand."

And in great rage, she took them all away from me. One daughter was fourteen years old, one twelve, and the other ten, but they were not old enough to be talked to about religion. Let them drift into the world and plunge into worldly amusements, and then see how hard it is to reach them.

Many a mother is mourning today because her boy has gone beyond her reach and will not allow her to pray with him. She may pray for him, but he will not let her pray or talk with him. In those early days when his mind was tender and young, she might have led him to Christ. Bring them in. *"Suffer the little children to come unto me, and forbid them not: for of such is the kingdom of God"* (Mark 10:14).

Is there a prayerless father reading this? May God let the arrow go down into your soul! Make up your mind that, with God helping you, you will get the children in. God's order is to the father first, but if he isn't true to his duty, then the mother should be true and save the children from the wreck. Now is the time to do it, while you have them under your roof. Exert your parental influence over them.

I never speak to parents without thinking of two fathers, one of whom lived on the banks of the Mississippi, the other in New York. The first one devoted all his time to amassing wealth. He had a son to whom he was much attached, and one day the boy was brought home badly injured. The father was informed that the boy would live only a short time, and he broke the news to his son as gently as possible.

"You say I cannot live, father? Oh! Then pray for my soul," said the boy.

In all those years, that father had never said a prayer for his son, and he told him he couldn't. Shortly after, the boy died. That father has since said that he would give all that he possessed if he could call that boy back only to offer one short prayer for him.

The other father had a boy who had been sick some time, and he came home one day and found his wife weeping. She said, "I cannot help but believe that this is going to prove fatal."

The man started and said, "If you think so, I wish you would tell him."

But the mother could not tell her son. The father went to the sick room, and he saw that death was imminent, and he said, "My son, do you know you are not going to live?"

The little fellow looked up and said, "No. Is this death that I feel stealing over me? Will I die today?"

"Yes, my son, you cannot live the day out."

And the little fellow smiled and said, "Well, father, I will be with Jesus tonight, won't I?"

"Yes, you will spend the night with the Lord," and the father broke down and wept.

The little fellow saw the tears, and said, "Don't weep for me. I will go to Jesus and tell Him that ever since I can remember, you have prayed for me."

I have three children, and if God would take them from me, I would rather have them take such a message home to Him than to have the wealth of the whole world. Oh! Would to God I could say something to stir you, fathers and mothers, to get your children into the ark.

❧5❧

Humility

"Learn of me; for I am meek and lowly in heart."
—Matthew 11:29

There is no harder lesson to learn than the lesson of humility. It is not taught in the schools of men, only in the school of Christ. It is the rarest of all the gifts. Very rarely do we find a man or woman who is following close to the footsteps of the Master in meekness and in humility. I believe that it is the hardest lesson that Jesus Christ had to teach His disciples while He was here on earth. At first, it looked as though He had failed to teach it to the twelve men who had been with Him almost constantly for three years.

I believe that if we are humble enough, we will be sure to get a great blessing. After all, I think that more depends on us than on the Lord, because He is always ready to give a blessing and give it freely, but we are not always in a position to receive it. He always blesses the humble, and, if we can get down in the dust before Him, no one will go away disappointed. It was Mary at the feet of Jesus who had chosen the better part.

Did you ever notice the reason Christ gave for learning about Him? He might have said, "Learn of me because I am the most advanced thinker of the age. I have performed miracles that no one else has performed. I have shown my supernatural power in a thousand ways." But no; the reason He gave was that He was *"meek and lowly in heart"* (Matthew 11:29).

We read of the three men in Scripture whose faces shone, and all three were noted for their meekness and humility. We are told that the face of Christ shone at His transfiguration. (See Matthew 17:1–2.) Moses, after he had been on the mount for forty days, came down from his communion with God with a shining face. (See Exodus 34:28–35.) When Stephen stood before the Sanhedrin on the day of his death, his face was lighted up with glory. (See Acts 6:8–15.) If our faces are to shine, we must get into the valley of humility; we must go down in the dust before God.

Bunyan said that it is hard to get down into the valley of humiliation; the descent into it is steep and rugged, but it is very fruitful and fertile and beautiful once we get there. I think that no one will dispute that; almost every man, even the ungodly, admires meekness.

Saint Augustine was once asked what was the first of the religious graces, and he said, "Humility." The, he was asked what was the second, and he replied, "Humility." He was asked the third, and he said, "Humility." I think that if we are humble, we have all the graces.

Some years ago, I saw what is called a sensitive plant. I happened to breathe on it, and suddenly it drooped its head. I touched it, and it withered away. Humility is as sensitive as that; it cannot safely be brought out on exhibition. A man who is flattering himself that he is humble and is walking close to the Master is self-deceived. It consists not in thinking infrequently of ourselves but in not thinking of ourselves at all. *"Moses wist not that the skin of his face shone"* (Exodus 34:29). If humility speaks of itself, it is gone.

Someone has said that the grass is an illustration of lowly grace. It was created for the lowliest service. Cut it, and it springs up again. The cattle feed on it, and yet how beautiful it is.

The showers fall upon the mountain peaks and very often leave them barren because the water rushes down into the meadows and valleys and makes the lowly places fertile. If a man is proud and lifted up, rivers of grace may flow over him and yet leave him barren and unfruitful while they bring blessing to the man who has been brought low by the grace of God.

A man can counterfeit love, he can counterfeit faith, he can counterfeit hope and all the other graces, but it is very difficult to counterfeit humility. You soon detect mock humility. They have a saying in the East among the

Arabs that as the tares and the wheat grow, they show which ones God has blessed. The ears that God has blessed bow their heads and acknowledge every grain, and the more fruitful they are, the lower their heads are bowed. The tares that God has sent as a curse lift up their heads erect, high above the wheat, but they are only fruitful in producing evil.

I have a pear tree on my farm that is very beautiful. It appears to be one of the most beautiful trees on my place. Every branch seems to be reaching up to the light and stands almost like a wax candle, but I never get any fruit from it. I have another tree that was so full of fruit last year that the branches almost touched the ground. If we only get down low enough, my friends, God will use every one of us to His glory.

As the lark that soars the highest builds her nest the lowest; as the nightingale that sings so sweetly sings in the shade when all things rest; as the branches that are most filled with fruit bend lowest; as the ship most laden sinks deepest in the water—so the holiest Christians are the humblest.

Your Victory in Jesus

Years ago, the *London Times* told the story of a petition that was being circulated for signatures. It was a time of great excitement, and this petition was intended to have great influence in the House of Lords. But there was one word left out. Instead of reading, "We humbly beseech thee," it read, "We beseech thee." So it was ruled out. My friends, if we want to make an appeal to the God of Heaven, we must humble ourselves, and if we do humble ourselves, we will not be disappointed.

As I have been studying some Bible characters who illustrate humility, I have been ashamed of myself. When I put my life beside the lives of some of those men, I say, "Shame on the Christianity of the present day." If you want to get a good idea of yourself, look at some of the Bible characters who have been clothed with meekness and humility, and see what a contrast your position is before God and man.

One of the meekest characters in history was John the Baptist. You remember that when they sent a delegation to him and asked if he was Elijah or this prophet or that prophet, he said, "No." Now, he might have said some very flattering things about himself. He might have said, "I am the son of the old priest Zacharias. Haven't you heard of my fame as a preacher? I have probably baptized more people than any man living. The world has never seen a preacher like me."

I honestly believe that in the present day, most men standing in his position would do that. On a train some time ago, I heard a man talking so loudly that all of the people in the car could hear him. He said that he had baptized more people than any man in his denomination. He told how many thousand miles he had traveled, how many sermons he had preached, how many open-air services he had held, and this and that, until I was so ashamed that I had to hide my head. This is the age of boasting. It is the day of the great "I."

My attention was recently called to the fact that in all the Psalms, you cannot find any place where David refers to his victory over the giant, Goliath. If it had been in the present day, there would have been a volume written about it at once. I don't know how many poems there would be telling of the great things that this man had done. He would have been in demand as a lecturer and would have added a title to his name: G.G.K., Great Giant Killer. That is how it is today: great evangelists, great preachers, great theologians, great bishops.

"John," they asked, "who are you?"

"I am nobody. I am to be heard, not to be seen; I am only a voice."

John the Baptist hadn't a word to say about himself. I once heard a little bird singing faintly close by me. At last, it got clear out of sight, and then its notes were still sweeter. The higher it flew, the sweeter its notes sounded. If we can only get self out of sight and learn from Him who was meek and lowly in heart, we will be lifted up into heavenly places.

The Gospel of Mark tells us that John came and preached, saying, *"There cometh one mightier than I after me, the latchet of whose shoes I am not worthy to stoop down and unloose"* (Mark 1:7). Think of that, and bear in mind that Christ was looked upon as a deceiver, a village carpenter. Yet here is John, the son of the old priest, who had a much higher position in the sight of men than that of Jesus. Great crowds were coming to hear him, and even Herod attended his meetings.

When his disciples came and told John that Christ was beginning to draw crowds, he nobly answered,

> *A man can receive nothing, except it be given him from heaven. Ye your-selves bear me witness, that I said, I am not the Christ, but that I am sent before him. He that hath the bride is the bridegroom: but the friend of the bridegroom, which standeth and heareth him, rejoiceth greatly because of the bridegroom's voice: this my joy therefore is fulfilled. He must increase, but I must decrease.*
> (John 3:27–30)

It is easy to read that, but it is hard for us to live in the power of it. It is very hard for us to be ready to decrease, to grow smaller and smaller, that Christ may increase. The morning star fades away when the sun rises.

He that cometh from above is above all: he that is of the earth is earthly, and speaketh of the earth: he that cometh from heaven is above all. And what he hath seen and heard, that he testifieth; and no man receiveth his testimony. He that hath received his testimony hath set to his seal that God is true. For he whom God hath sent speaketh the words of God: for God giveth not the Spirit by measure unto him. (John 3:31–34)

Let us now turn the light upon ourselves. Have we been decreasing of late? Do we think less of ourselves and of our position than we did a year ago? Are we seeking to obtain some position of dignity? Are we wanting to hold on to some title, and are we offended because we are not treated with the courtesy that we think is due us?

Some time ago, I heard a man in the pulpit say that he should take offense if he was not addressed by his title. My dear friend, are you going to take the position that you must have a title and you must have every letter addressed with the title or you will be offended? John did not want any title, and when we are right with God, we will not be caring about titles.

In one of his early epistles, Paul called himself the *"least of the apostles"* (1 Corinthians 15:9). Later on he claimed to be *"less than the least of all saints"* (Ephesians 3:8), and again, just before his death, humbly declared that he was the chief of sinners. (See 1 Timothy 1:15). Notice how he seemed to have grown smaller and smaller in his own estimation. So it was with John. And I do hope and pray that as the days go by, we may feel like hiding ourselves and letting God have all the honor and glory.

"When I look back upon my own religious experience," said Andrew Murray, "or round upon the church of Christ in the world, I stand amazed at the thought of how little humility is sought after as the distinguishing feature of the discipleship of Jesus. In preaching and living, in the daily communication of the home and social life, in the more special fellowship with Christians, in the direction and performance of work for Christ—alas, how much proof there is that humility is not esteemed the cardinal virtue, the only root from which the graces can grow, the one indispensable condition of true fellowship with Jesus."

See what Christ said about John: *"He was a burning and a shining light"* (John 5:35). Christ gave him the honor that belonged to him. If you take a humble position, Christ will see it. If you want God to help you, then take a low position.

I am afraid that if we had been in John's place, many of us would have said, "What did Christ say—'I am a burning and shining light'?" Then we would have had that compliment put in the newspapers and would have sent them to our friends with that part marked in blue pencil. Sometimes I get a letter just full of clippings from the newspapers stating that this man is more eloquent than Gough, etc. And the man wants me to get him into a church. Do you think that a man who has such eloquence would be looking for a church?

No, they would all be looking for him. My dear friends, isn't it humiliating? Sometimes I think it is a wonder that any man is converted these days. Let another praise you. Don't go around praising yourself. If we want God to lift us up, let us get down. The lower we get, the higher God will lift us. Christ's eulogy of John is as follows: *"For I say unto you, Among those that are born of women there is not a greater prophet than John the Baptist"* (Luke 7:28).

There is a story told of William Carey, the great missionary, that he was invited by the Governor General of India to go to a dinner party at which there were some aristocratic military officers who looked down upon missionaries with scorn and contempt.

One of these officers said at the table, "I believe that Carey was a shoemaker, wasn't he, before he took up the profession of a missionary?"

Mr. Carey spoke up and said, "Oh no, I was only a cobbler. I could mend shoes and wasn't ashamed of it."

The one prominent virtue of Christ, next to His obedience, is His humility, and even His obedience grew out of His humility.

Who, being in the form of God, thought it not robbery to be equal with God: but made himself of no reputation, and took upon him the form of a servant, and was made in the likeness of men: and being found in fashion as a man, he humbled himself, and became obedient unto death, even the death of the cross. (Philippians 2:6–8)

In His lowly birth, His submission to His earthly parents, His seclusion during thirty years, His consorting with the poor and despised, and His entire submission and dependence upon His Father, this virtue that was completed in His death on the cross, shines out.

One day, Jesus was on His way to Capernaum and was talking about His coming death and suffering and about His resurrection, and He heard quite a heated discussion going on behind Him. When He came into the house at Capernaum, He turned to His disciples and said, *"What was it that ye disputed among yourselves by the way?"* (Mark 9:33).

I can almost see John looking at James and Peter at Andrew, and they all look ashamed. *"Who should be the greatest"* (Mark 9:34). That discussion has wrecked party after party, one society after another: "Who will be the greatest?"

The way Christ took to teach them humility was by putting a little child in their midst and saying, *"Whosoever shall receive one of such children in my name, receiveth me: and whosoever shall receive me, receiveth not me, but him that sent me"* (Mark 9:37).

To me, one of the saddest things in the life of Jesus Christ was the fact that just before His crucifixion, His disciples were striving to see who would be the greatest. That night, He instituted the Supper, and they ate the Passover together. It was His last night on earth, and they never saw Him so sorrowful before. He knew Judas was going to sell Him for thirty pieces of silver. He knew that Peter would deny Him. And yet, in addition to this, when going into the very shadow of the cross, there arose this strife as to who would be the greatest. He took a towel and girded

Himself like a slave, and He took a basin of water and stooped and washed their feet. That was another object lesson of humility. He said, *"Ye call me Master and Lord: and ye say well; for so I am. If I then, your Lord and Master, have washed your feet; ye also ought to wash one another's feet"* (John 13:13–14).

When the Holy Spirit came and those men were filled, mark the difference from that time on. Matthew took up his pen to write, and he kept Matthew out of sight. He told what Peter and Andrew did, but he called himself Matthew *"the publican."* (See Matthew 10:3.) He told how they left all to follow Christ but did not mention the feast he gave. Jerome said that Mark's Gospel is to be regarded as memoirs of Peter's discourses and to have been published by his authority. Yet here we constantly find that damaging things are mentioned about Peter and things to his credit are not referred to. Mark's Gospel omits all allusion to Peter's faith in venturing on the sea but goes into detail about the story of his fall and denial of our Lord. Peter put himself down and lifted others up.

If Luke's Gospel had been written today, it would be signed by the great Dr. Luke, and you would have his photograph as a frontispiece. But you can't find Luke's name; he kept out of sight. He wrote two books, and his name is not to be found in either. John covered himself under the expression, *"the disciple whom Jesus loved"* (John 21:20). None of the four men whom history and tradition assert to be the authors of the Gospels lay claim to the authorship of their writings. Dear children of God, I wish that I had the same spirit, that I could just get out of sight and hide myself.

My dear friends, I believe our only hope is to be filled with the Spirit of Christ. May God fill us, so that we will be filled with meekness and humility. Let us take the hymn, "O, to be nothing, nothing," and make it the language of our hearts. It breathes the spirit of Him who said, *"The Son can do **nothing** of himself"* (John 5:19, emphasis added).

> *Oh, to be nothing, nothing!*
> *Only to lie at His feet,*
> *A broken and emptied vessel,*

For the Master's use made meet,
Emptied, that He might fill me
As forth to His service I go;
Broken, that so unhindered,
His life through me might flow.

☙6❧

Rest

Some years ago, a gentleman came to me and asked me which promise I thought was the most precious of all those that Christ left. I took some time to look them over, but I gave it up. I found that I could not answer the question.

It is like a man with a large family of children: He cannot tell which he likes best; he loves them all. But if not the best, this is one of the sweetest promises of all:

> Come unto me, all ye that labour and are heavy laden, and I will give you rest. Take my yoke upon you, and learn of me; for I am meek and lowly in heart: and ye shall find rest unto

*your souls. For my yoke is easy, and
my burden is light.*
(Matthew 11:28–30)

There are a good many people who think
the promises are not going to be fulfilled.
There are some that you do see fulfilled, and
you cannot help but believe they are true.
Now remember that all the promises are not
given without conditions. Some are given
with conditions attached to them, and others
without. For instance, Psalm 66:18 says, *"If I
regard iniquity in my heart, the Lord will not
hear me."* Now, I need not pray as long as I
am cherishing some known sin. He will not
hear me, much less answer me. The Lord says
in Psalm 84:11, *"No good thing will he with-
hold from them that walk uprightly."* If I am
not walking uprightly, I have no claims under
the promise.

Again, some of the promises were made
to certain individuals or nations. For instance,
God said He would make Abraham's seed
multiply as the stars of heaven, but that is not
a promise for you or me. Some promises made
to the Jews do not apply to the Gentiles.

Then, there are promises without conditions. He promised Adam and Eve that the world would have a Savior, and there was no power in earth or perdition that could keep Christ from coming at the appointed time. When Christ left the world, He said He would send us the Holy Spirit. He had only been gone ten days when the Holy Spirit came. So you can run right through the Scriptures, and you will find that some of the promises are with, and some without, conditions. If we don't comply with the conditions, we cannot expect the promises to be fulfilled.

I believe it will be the experience of all men and women on the face of the earth to testify in the evening of life that if they have complied with the condition, the Lord has fulfilled His Word to the letter. Joshua, the old Hebrew hero, was an illustration. After having tested God forty years in the Egyptian brick kilns, forty years in the desert, and thirty years in the Promised Land, his dying testimony was, *"Not one thing hath failed of all the good things which the LORD your God spake concerning you"* (Joshua 23:14). I believe you could have the ocean dry up more easily than break one of God's promises. So when we come to a promise like the one we have before us now, I want you to bear in mind that it cannot be diminished. *"Come unto me, all ye that labour and are heavy laden, and I will give you rest"* (Matthew 11:28).

Perhaps you say, "I hope Mr. Moody is not going to preach on this old text." Yes, I am. When I pick up an album, it does not interest me if all the photographs are new, but if I know any of the faces, I stop at once. So with these old, well-known texts. They have quenched our thirst before, but the water is still bubbling up—we cannot drink it dry.

If you probe the human heart, you will find a need, and that need is rest. The cry of the world today is, "Where can rest be found?" Why are theaters and places of amusement crowded at night? What is the secret of Sunday driving, of the saloons and brothels? Some think they are going to find rest in pleasure, others think they are going to get it in wealth, and others in literature. They are seeking, and yet they are finding no rest.

Where Can Rest Be Found?

If I wanted to find a person who had rest, I would not go among the very wealthy. The man in the twelfth chapter of Luke thought he was going to get rest by multiplying his goods, but he was disappointed. *"Soul...take thine ease"* (verse 19). I venture to say that there is not a person in this wide world who has tried to find rest in that way and found it. Money cannot buy it. Many wealthy people would gladly give millions if they could purchase rest as they do their stocks and shares. God has made the soul a little too large for this world. Roll the whole world in, and still there is room. There is care in getting wealth and more care in keeping it.

Nor would I go among the pleasure seekers. They have a few hours' enjoyment, but the next day there is enough sorrow to counterbalance it. They may drink the cup of pleasure today, but the cup of pain comes tomorrow.

To find rest, I would never go among the politicians or among the so-called great. Congress is the last place on earth that I would go. In the Lower House they want to go to the Senate; in the Senate they want to go to the Cabinet; then they want to go to the White House, and rest has never been found there. Nor would I go among the halls of learning. *"Much study is a weariness of the flesh"* (Ecclesiastes 12:12).

I would not go among the upper ten, the upper class, for they are constantly chasing after fashion. Have you not noticed their troubled faces on our streets? And the face is an index to the soul. They have no hopeful look. Their worship of pleasure is slavery. Solomon tried pleasure and found bitter disappointment, and down the ages has come the bitter cry, *"All is vanity"* (Ecclesiastes 1:2).

No, there is no rest in sin. The wicked know nothing about it. Scripture tells us, *"The wicked are like the troubled sea, when it cannot rest"* (Isaiah 57:20). You have perhaps been on the sea when it is calm, when the water is as clear as crystal, and it seemed as if the sea were at rest. But if you looked closely, you would see that the waves were still coming in and that the calm was only on the surface. Man, like the sea, has no rest. He has had no rest since Adam fell, and there is none for him until he returns to God again and the light of Christ shines into his heart.

Rest cannot be found in the world, and, thank God, the world cannot take it from the believing heart! Sin is the cause of all this unrest. It brought toil and labor and misery into the world.

Now for something positive. I would go successfully to someone who has heard the sweet voice of Jesus and has laid his burden down at the cross. There is rest, sweet rest. Thousands could testify to this blessed fact. They could truthfully say,

> *I heard the voice of Jesus say,*
> *"Come unto me and rest.*
> *Lay down, thou weary one, lay down,*
> *Thy head upon my breast."*
> *I came to Jesus as I was,*
> *Weary and worn and sad.*
> *I found in Him a resting place,*
> *And He hath made me glad.*

Among all his writings, Saint Augustine has nothing sweeter than this: "Thou hast made us for Thyself, O God, and our heart is restless till it rests in Thee."

Do you know that for four thousand years, no prophet or priest or patriarch ever stood up and uttered a text like this? It would be blasphemy for Moses to have uttered a text like it. Do you think he had rest when he was teasing the Lord to let him go into the Promised Land? Do you think Elijah could have uttered such a text as this when, under the juniper tree, he prayed that he might die?

And this is one of the strongest proofs that Jesus Christ was not only man but also God. He was God-man, and this is heaven's proclamation: *"Come unto me...and I will give you rest"* (Matthew 11:28). He brought it down from heaven with Him.

Now, if this text were not true, don't you think it would have been found out by this time? I believe it as much as I believe in my existence. Why? Because I not only find it in the Book but also in my own experience. The

"I wills" of Christ have never been broken and never can be.

I thank God for the word *"give"* in that passage; He doesn't sell it. Some of us are so poor that we could not buy rest if it were for sale. Thank God, we can get it for nothing.

I like to have a text like this because it takes us all in. *"Come unto me, **all** ye that labour"* (Matthew 11:28, emphasis added). That doesn't mean a select few refined ladies and cultured men. It doesn't mean good people only. It applies to saint and sinner alike. Hospitals are for the sick, not for healthy people. Do you think that Christ would shut the door in someone's face, and say, "I did not mean all; I only meant certain ones"? If you cannot come as a saint, come as a sinner. Only come!

A lady once told me that she was so hard-hearted she couldn't come.

"Well," I said, "my good woman, it doesn't say 'all ye soft-hearted people come.' Black hearts, vile hearts, hard hearts, soft hearts, all hearts come. Who can soften your hard heart but Himself?"

The harder the heart, the more need you have to come. If my watch stops, I don't take it to a drugstore or to a blacksmith's shop but to the watchmaker's to have it repaired. So if the heart gets out of order, take it to its keeper, Christ, to have it set right. If you can prove that you are a sinner, you are entitled to the promise. Get all the benefit you can out of it.

Now, there are a good many believers who think this text applies only to sinners. It is just the thing for them, too. What do we see today? The church, Christian people, all loaded down with cares and troubles. *"Come unto me, all ye that labour"* (Matthew 11:28). All! I believe that includes the Christian whose heart is burdened with some great sorrow. The Lord wants you to come.

Christ, the Burden Bearer

The Bible says in another place, *"Casting all your care upon him; for he careth for you"* (1 Peter 5:7). We would have a victorious church if we could get Christian people to realize that. But they have never made the discovery. They agree that Christ is the Sin

Bearer, but they do not realize that He is also the Burden Bearer. *"Surely he hath borne our griefs, and carried our sorrows"* (Isaiah 53:4). It is the privilege of every child of God to walk in unclouded sunlight.

Some people go back into the past and rake up all the troubles they ever had. Then they look into the future and anticipate that they will have still more trouble, and they go reeling and staggering all through life. They give you the cold chills every time they meet you. They put on a whining voice and tell you what a hard time they have had. I believe they embalm their troubles and bring out the mummy on every opportunity. The Lord tells us to cast all our cares on Him. He wants to carry our burdens and our troubles. What we need is a joyful church, and we are not going to convert the world until we have it. We want to get this long-faced Christianity off the face of the earth.

Take these people who have some great burden, and let them come into a meeting. If you can focus their attention on the singing or preaching, they will say, "Oh, wasn't it grand! I forgot all my cares." And they just drop their bundle at the end of the pew. But the moment the benediction is pronounced, they grab the bundle again. You laugh, but you do it yourself. Cast your care on Him.

Sometimes they go into their closets and close their doors, and they get so carried away and lifted up that they forget their troubles. But they just take them up again the moment they get off their knees. Leave your sorrow now; cast all your cares upon Him. If you cannot come to Christ as a saint, come as a sinner. But if you are a saint with some trouble or care, bring it to Him. Saint and sinner, come! He wants you all. Don't let Satan deceive you into believing that you cannot come if you will. Christ says, *"Ye will not come to me"* (John 5:40). With the command comes the power.

A man in one of our meetings in Europe said he would like to come, but he was chained and couldn't come. A Scotsman said to him, "Aye, man, why don't you come chain and all?"

He said, "I never thought of that."

Are you cross and peevish, and do you make things unpleasant at home? My friend, come to Christ and ask Him to help you. Whatever the sin is, bring it to Him.

What Does It Mean to Come?

Perhaps you said, "Mr. Moody, I wish you would tell us what it is to come." I have given up trying to explain it. I always feel like the minister who said he was going to *confound*, instead of *expound*, the chapter.

The best definition is just "come." The more you try to explain it, the more you are mystified. About the first thing a mother teaches her child is to look. She takes the baby to the window, and she says, "Look, baby, Papa is coming!" Then she teaches the child to come. She props him up against a chair and says, "Come!" and, by and by, the little thing pushes the chair along toward mama. That's coming. You don't need to go to college to learn how. You don't need any minister to tell you what it is. Now, will you come to Christ? He said, *"Him that cometh to me I will in no wise cast out"* (John 6:37).

When we have such a promise as this, let us cling to it and never give it up. Christ is not mocking us. He wants us to come with all our sins and backslidings and throw ourselves upon His bosom. It is our sins God wants, not our tears only. They alone do no good. And we cannot come through resolutions. Action is necessary. How many times at church have we said, "I will turn over a new leaf," but the Monday leaf is worse than the Saturday leaf?

The way to heaven is as straight as a ruler, but it is by the way of the cross. Don't try to get around it. Should I tell you what the *"yoke"* referred to in the text is? (See Matthew 11:29–30.) It is the cross that Christians must bear. The only way by which you can find rest in this dark world is by taking up the yoke of Christ. I do not know what it may include in your case beyond taking up your Christian duties, acknowledging Christ, and acting as becomes one of His disciples. Perhaps it may be to erect a family altar, to tell a godless husband that you have made up your mind to serve God, or to tell your parents that you want to be a Christian. Follow the will of God, and happiness and peace and rest will come. The way of obedience is always the way of blessing.

I was preaching in Chicago to a hall full of women one Sunday afternoon. After the meeting was over, a lady came to me and said she wanted to talk to me. She said she would accept Christ, and after some conversation, she went home. I looked for her for a whole week but didn't see her until the following Sunday afternoon. She came and sat down right in front of me, and her face had such a sad expression. She seemed to have entered into the misery, instead of the joy, of the Lord.

After the meeting was over, I went to her and asked her what the trouble was.

She said, "Oh, Mr. Moody, this has been the most miserable week of my life."

I asked her if there was anyone with whom she had had trouble and whom she could not forgive.

She said, "No, not that I know of."

"Well, did you tell your friends about having found the Savior?"

"Indeed I didn't; I have been all the week trying to keep it from them."

"Well," I said, "that is the reason why you have no peace."

She wanted to take the crown but did not want the cross. My friends, you must go by the way of Calvary. If you ever get rest, you must get it at the foot of the cross.

"Why," she said, "if I should go home and tell my infidel husband that I had found Christ, I don't know what he would do. I think he would turn me out."

"Well," I said, "go out."

She went away timid and pale, promising that she would tell him because she did not want another wretched week. She was bound to have peace.

The next night I gave a lecture to men only, and in the hall there were eight thousand men and one solitary woman. When I got through and went into the inquiry room, I found this lady with her husband. She introduced him to me—he was a doctor and a very influential man—and said, "He wants to become a Christian."

I took my Bible and told him all about Christ, and he accepted Him. I said to her after it was all over, "It turned out quite differently from what you expected, didn't it?"

"Yes," she replied, "I was never so scared in my life. I expected he would do something dreadful, but it has turned out so well."

She took God's way and got rest.

I want to say to young ladies, perhaps you have a godless father or mother, a skeptical brother who is going down through drink, and perhaps there is no one who can reach them but you. How many times a pure, godly young lady has taken the light into some darkened home! Many homes might be lit up with the Gospel if the mothers and daughters would only speak the Word.

The last time Mr. Ira Sankey and I were in Edinburgh, there was a family—a father, two sisters, and a brother—who every morning would take the morning paper and pick my sermon to pieces. They were indignant to think that the Edinburgh people should be carried away with such preaching.

One day, one of the sisters was going by the hall where a meeting was being held, and she thought she would drop in to see what class of people went there. She happened to take a seat by a godly lady who said to her, "I hope you are interested in this work."

She tossed her head and said, "Indeed, I am not. I am disgusted with everything I have seen and heard."

"Well," said the lady, "perhaps you came prejudiced."

"Yes, and the meeting has not removed any of it but has rather increased it."

"I have received a good deal of good from them."

"There is nothing here for me. I don't see how an intellectual person can be interested."

To make a long story short, when the meeting broke up, just a little of the prejudice had worn away. She promised to come back again the next day, and then she attended three or four more meetings and became quite interested. She said nothing to her family until finally the burden became too heavy, and she told them. They laughed at her and made her the butt of their ridicule.

One day, the two sisters were together, and the other said, "Now what have you got at those meetings that you didn't have in the first place?"

"I have a peace that I never knew of before. I am at peace with God, myself, and all the world." Did you ever have a little war of your own with your neighbors or your own family? She continued, "I have self-control. You know, Sister, if you had said half the mean things before I was converted that you have said since, I would have been angry and answered back, but if you remember correctly, I haven't answered once since I have been converted."

The sister said, "You certainly have something that I have not." The other told her it was for her, too, and she brought the sister to the meetings where she found peace.

Like Martha and Mary, they had a brother, but he was a member of the University of Edinburgh. Could he be converted? Would he go to these meetings? No! It might do for women but not for him. One night they came home and told him that a chum of his own, a member of the University, had stood up and confessed Christ. When he sat down, his brother got up and confessed and so with the third one. When the young man heard it, he said, "Do you mean to tell me that he has been converted?"

"Yes."

"Well," he said, "there must be something in it."

He put on his hat and coat and went to see his friend, Black. Black got him to go down to the meetings, and he was converted.

We went through to Glasgow and had not been there six weeks when news came that that young man had been stricken down and had died. When he was dying, he had called his father to his bedside and said, "Wasn't it a good thing that my sisters went to those meetings? Won't you meet me in heaven, father?"

"Yes, my son, I am so glad you are a Christian; that is the only comfort that I have in losing you. I will become a Christian and will meet you again."

I tell this to encourage some sister to go home and carry the message of salvation. It may be that your brother will be taken away in a few months. My dear friends, are we not living in solemn days? Isn't it time for us to get our friends into the kingdom of God? Come, wife, won't you tell your husband? Come, sister, won't you tell your brother? Won't you take up your cross now? The blessing of God will rest on your soul if you will.

I was in Wales once, and a lady told me this little story: An English friend of hers, a mother, had a child who was sick. At first, they thought there was no danger, until one day, the doctor came in and said that the symptoms were very unfavorable. He took the mother out of the room and told her that the child could not live. It came like a thunderbolt. After the doctor had gone, the mother went into the room where the child lay and began to talk to the child and tried to divert her mind.

"Darling, do you know you will soon hear the music of heaven? You will hear a sweeter song than you have ever heard on earth. You will hear them sing the song of Moses and the Lamb. You are very fond of music. Won't it be sweet, darling?"

And the tired, sick little girl turned her head away and said, "Oh, Mama, I am so tired and so sick that I think it would make me worse to hear all that music."

"Well," the mother said, "you will see Jesus. You will see the seraphim and cherubim and the streets all paved with gold," and she went on picturing heaven as it is described in Revelation.

The little tired child again turned her head away and said, "Oh, Mama, I am so tired that I think it would make me worse to see all those beautiful things!"

At last, the mother took the child up in her arms and pressed her to her loving heart. And that little sick one whispered, "Oh, Mama, that is what I want. If Jesus will only take me in His arms and let me rest!"

Dear friend, are you not tired and weary of sin? Are you not weary of the turmoil of life? You can find rest on the bosom of the Son of God.

ᴥ7ᴥ

Seven "I Wills" of Christ

A man, when he says, "I will," may not mean much. We very often say, "I will," when we don't mean to fulfill what we say, but when we come to the "I will" of Christ, He means to fulfill it. Everything He has promised to do, He is able and willing to accomplish, and He is going to do it. I cannot find any passage in Scripture in which He says, "I will" do this or "I will" do that, in which it is not done.

The "I Will" of Salvation

The first "I will" to which I want to direct your attention is found in John 6:37: *"Him that cometh to me I will in no wise cast out."*

I imagine someone might say, "Well, if I was what I ought to be, I would come; but when my mind goes over the past record of my life, it is too dark. I am not fit to come."

You must bear in mind that Jesus Christ came to save not good people, not the upright and just, but sinners like you and me who have gone astray and sinned and come short of the glory of God.

Listen to this "I will." It goes right into the heart: *"Him that cometh to me I will in no wise cast out"* (John 6:37). Surely that is broad enough—is it not? I don't care who the person is. Whatever his trials, his troubles, his sorrows, or his sins may be, if he will only come straight to the Master, He will not cast him out. Come then, poor sinner, come just as you are, and take Him at His word.

He is so anxious to save sinners that He will take everyone who comes. He will take those who are so full of sin that they are despised by all who know them, those who have been rejected by their fathers and mothers, those who have been cast off by the wives of their bosoms. He will take those who have sunk so low that upon them no eye of pity is cast. His occupation is to hear and save. That is what He left heaven and came into the world for. That is what He left the throne of God for—to save sinners. *"For the Son of man is come to seek and to save that which was lost"* (Luke 19:10). He did not come to condemn the world but to save the world through Himself. (See John 3:17.)

A wild and prodigal young man who was running headlong into ruin came to one of our meetings in Chicago. The Spirit of God got hold of him. While I was conversing with him and endeavoring to bring him to Christ, I quoted the above verse to him.

I asked him, "Do you believe Christ said that?"

"I suppose He did."

"Suppose He did! Do you believe it?"

"I hope so."

"Hope so! Do you believe it? You do your work, and the Lord will do His. Just come as you are, and throw yourself upon His bosom, and He will not cast you out."

This man thought it was too simple and easy. At last, light seemed to break in upon him, and he seemed to find comfort from it. It was past midnight before he got down on his knees, but down he went and was converted.

I said, "Now, don't think you are going to get out of the devil's territory without trouble. The devil will come to you tomorrow morning and say it was all feeling, that you only imagined you were accepted by God. When he does, don't fight him with your own opinions, but fight him with John 6:37: *"Him that cometh to me I will in no wise cast out."* Let that be the *'sword of the Spirit.'"* (See Ephesians 6:17.)

I don't believe that any man ever starts to go to Christ without the devil striving somehow or other to meet him and trip him up. And even after he has come to Christ, the devil tries to assail him with doubts and make him believe there is something wrong in it.

The struggle came sooner than I thought in this man's case. When he was on his way home, the devil assailed him. He used this text, but the devil put this thought into his mind: "How do you know Christ ever said that after all? Perhaps the translators made a mistake."

Into darkness he went again. He was in trouble until about two o'clock in the morning. At last, he came to this conclusion. He said, "I will believe it anyway, and when I get to heaven, if it isn't true, I will just tell the Lord I didn't make the mistake—the translators made it."

The kings and princes of this world, when they issue invitations, call around them the rich, the mighty and powerful, the honorable, and the wise. But the Lord, when He was on earth, called around Him the vilest of the vile. That was the principal fault the people found with Him. Those self-righteous Pharisees were not going to associate with prostitutes and tax collectors. The principal charge against Him was, *"This man receiveth sinners, and eateth with them"* (Luke 15:2).

Who would have such a man around him as John Bunyan in his time? He, a Bedford tinker, couldn't get inside one of the princely castles. I was very much amused when I was over on the other side of the Atlantic. They had erected a monument to John Bunyan, and it was unveiled by lords and dukes and great men. While Bunyan was on earth, they would not have allowed him inside the walls of their castles. Yet he was made one of the mightiest instruments in the spread of the Gospel. No book that has ever been written comes as near to the Bible as John Bunyan's *Pilgrim's Progress*, and he was a poor Bedford tinker. So it is with God. He picks up some poor, lost tramp and makes him an instrument to turn hundreds and thousands to Christ.

George Whitefield, standing in his tabernacle in London and with a multitude gathered about him, cried out, "The Lord Jesus will save the devil's castaways!"

Two poor, abandoned wretches standing outside in the street heard him as his silvery voice rang out on the air. Looking into each other's faces, they said, "That must mean you and me." They wept and rejoiced. They drew near and looked in the door at the face of the earnest messenger who had tears streaming from his eyes as he pleaded with the people to give their hearts to God. One of these poor wretches wrote him a little note and sent it to him. Later that day, as he sat at the table of his friend Lady Huntington, someone present said, "Mr. Whitefield, did you not go a little too far today when you said that the Lord would save the devil's castaways?"

Taking the note from his pocket, he gave it to the lady, and said, "Will you read that note aloud?"

She read, "Mr. Whitefield: Two poor, lost women stood outside your tabernacle today and heard you say that the Lord would save the devil's castaways. We seized upon that as our last hope, and we write you this to tell you that we rejoice now in believing in Him, and from this good hour we will endeavor to serve Him who has done so much for us."

The "I Will" of Cleansing

The next "I will" is found in the fifth chapter of Luke:

> *And it came to pass, when he [Jesus] was in a certain city, behold a man full of leprosy: who seeing Jesus fell*

*on his face, and besought him, saying,
Lord, if thou wilt, thou canst make me
clean. And he put forth his hand, and
touched him, saying, I will: be thou
clean. And immediately the leprosy
departed from him.* (Luke 5:12–13)

Now, if any man or woman full of the
leprosy of sin reads this, if you will but go
to the Master and tell your case to Him, He
will speak to you as He did to that poor leper
and say, *"I will: be thou clean,"* and the leprosy of your sins will flee away from you. It is
the Lord, and the Lord alone, who can forgive
sins.

If you say to Him, "Lord, I am full of sin;
You can make me clean"—"Lord, I have a terrible temper; You can make me clean"—"Lord,
I have a deceitful heart. Cleanse me, oh Lord;
give me a new heart. Oh, Lord, give me the
power to overcome the flesh and the snares
of the devil!"—Lord, I am full of unclean
habits"—and if you come to Him with a sin-
cere spirit, you will hear the voice, *"I will: be
thou clean."* It will be done. If the God who
created the world out of nothing—who by a

breath put life into the world—says, "you will be clean," do you think you will not?

Now, you can make a wonderful exchange today. You can have health in the place of sickness; you can get rid of everything that is vile and hateful in the sight of God. The Son of God will come down and tell us that He will take away our leprosy and give us health in its stead. He will clothe us with the garments of salvation.

Is it not wonderful? That's what He means when He says, "I will." Oh, lay hold of this "I will"!

The "I Will" of Confession

Now turn to Matthew 10:32: *"Whosoever therefore shall confess me before men, him will I confess also before my Father which is in heaven."* There's the "I will" of confession.

That's the next thing that takes place after a man is saved. When we have been washed in the blood of the Lamb, the next thing is to get our mouths opened. We have to confess Christ here in this dark world and tell others about His love. We are not to be ashamed of the Son of God.

A man thinks it a great honor when he has achieved a victory that causes his name to be mentioned in the English Parliament or in the presence of the Queen and her court. How excited we used to be during the Civil War when some general did something extraordinary and when someone got up in Congress to confess his exploits. How the papers used to talk about it! In China, we read, the highest ambition of the successful soldier is to have his name written in the palace or temple of Confucius. But just think of having your name mentioned in the kingdom of heaven by the Prince of Glory, by the Son of God, because you confess Him here on earth! If you confess Him here, He will confess you up yonder.

If you wish to be brought into the clear light of liberty, you must take your stand on Christ's side. I have known many Christians to go groping about in darkness and never get into the clear light of the kingdom because they were ashamed to confess the Son of God. We are living in a day when men want a religion without the cross. They want the crown but not the cross. But if we are to be disciples of Jesus Christ, we have to take up our crosses daily, not once a year or on the Sabbath, but daily. And if we take up our crosses and follow Him, we will be blessed in the very act.

I remember a man in New York who used to come and pray with me. He had his cross. He was afraid to confess Christ. It seemed that down at the bottom of his trunk he had a Bible. He wanted to get it out and read it to the companion with whom he lived, but he was ashamed to do it. For a whole week, that was his cross, and after he had carried the burden that long and after a terrible struggle, he made up his mind. He said, "I will take my Bible out tonight and read it." He took it out, and soon he heard the footsteps of his friend coming upstairs.

His first impulse was to put it away again, but then he thought he would not—he would face his companion with it. His friend came in and, seeing him at his Bible, said, "John, are you interested in these things?"

"Yes," he replied.

"How long has this been, then?" asked his companion.

"Exactly a week," he answered. "For a whole week I have tried to get out my Bible to read to you, but I have never done so until now."

"Well," said his friend, "it is a strange thing. I was converted on the same night, and I too was ashamed to take my Bible out."

You are ashamed to take your Bible out and say, "I have lived a godless life for all these years, but I will commence now to live a life of righteousness." You are ashamed to open your Bible and read that blessed Psalm, *"The LORD is my shepherd; I shall not want"* (Psalm 23:1). You are ashamed to be seen on your knees. No man can be a disciple of Jesus Christ without bearing His cross. A great many people want to know why it is Jesus Christ has so few disciples while Muhammad has so many. The reason is that Muhammad gives no cross to bear. There are so few men who will come out to take their stand.

During the Civil War, I was struck by the great number of men who could go to the cannon's mouth without trembling but did not have courage to take up their Bibles and read them at night. They were ashamed of the Gospel of Jesus Christ, which *"is the power of God unto salvation"* (Romans 1:16).

> *Whosoever therefore shall confess me before men, him will I confess also before my Father which is in heaven. But whosoever shall deny me before men, him will I also deny before my Father which is in heaven.*
> (Matthew 10:32–33)

The "I Will" of Service

The next "I will" is the "I will" of service. There are a good many Christians who have been roused to say, "I want to do some service for Christ." Well, as Christ said to His disciples, *"Follow me, and I will make you fishers of men"* (Matthew 4:19).

There is no Christian who cannot help to bring someone to the Savior. Christ said, *"And I, if I be lifted up from the earth, will draw all men unto me"* (John 12:32), and our business is just to lift up Christ.

Our Lord said to Peter, *"Follow me, and I will make you fishers of men"* (Matthew 4:19), and Peter simply obeyed Him. There, on that day of Pentecost, we see the result. Peter had a good haul on the day of Pentecost. I doubt if he ever caught as many fish in one day as he did men on that day. It would have broken every net they had on board if they had had to drag up three thousand fishes.

I once read a man who took passage in a stagecoach. There were first-, second-, and third-class passengers. But when he looked into the coach, he saw all the passengers sitting together without distinction. He could not understand it until by and by, they came to a hill and the coach stopped. The driver called out, "First-class passengers keep their seats, second-class passengers get out and walk, third-class passengers get behind and push."

Now, in the church, we have no room for first-class passengers—people who think that salvation means an easy ride all the way to heaven. We have no room for second-class passengers—people who are carried most of the time and who, when they must work out their own salvation, go trudging on, never giving a thought to helping their fellows along. All church members ought to be third-class passengers—ready to dismount and push with a will, all together. That was John Wesley's definition of a church: "All at it, and always at it."

Every Christian ought to be a worker. He need not be a preacher, he need not be an evangelist, to be useful. He may be useful in business. See what power an employer has, if he likes! He could labor with his employees and in his business relations! Often a man can be far more useful in a business sphere than he could in another.

There is one reason, and a great reason, why so many do not succeed. I have been asked by a great many good men, "Why is it we don't have any results? We work hard, pray hard, and preach hard, and yet the success does not come." I will tell you. It is because they spend all their time mending their nets. No wonder they never catch anything.

The great matter is to hold inquiry meetings, and thus pull the net in, and see if you have caught anything. If you are always mending and setting the net, you won't catch many fish. Whoever heard of a man going out to fish and setting his net, and then letting it stop there, never pulling it in? Everybody would laugh at the man's folly.

A minister in England came to me one day and said, "I wish you would tell me why we ministers don't succeed better than we do."

I brought before him this idea of pulling in the net, and I said, "You ought to pull in your nets. There are many ministers in Manchester who can preach much better than I can, but I pull in the net."

Many people have objections to inquiry meetings, but I urged upon him the importance of them. The minister said, "I never did pull in my net, but I will try next Sunday."

He did so, and eight persons, anxious inquirers, went into his study. The next Sunday he came down to see me and said he had never had such a Sunday in his life. He had met with marvelous blessing. The next time he drew the net, there were forty; and when he came to see me later, he said to me joyfully, "Moody, I have had eight hundred conversions this last year! It is a great mistake I did not begin to pull in the net earlier."

So, my friends, if you want to catch men, just pull in the net. If you only catch one, it will be something. It may be a little child, but I have known a little child to convert a whole family. You don't know what is in that little dull-headed boy in the inquiry room; he may become a Martin Luther, a reformer who will make the world tremble. You cannot tell. God uses the weak things of this world to confound the mighty.

God's promise is as good as a banknote, "I promise to pay so-and-so," and here is one of Christ's promissory notes: *"Follow me, and I will make you fishers of men"* (Matthew 4:19). Will you not lay hold of the promise and trust it and follow Him now?

If a man preaches the Gospel, and preaches it faithfully, he ought to expect results then and there. I believe it is the privilege of God's children to reap the fruit of their labor, 365 days a year.

"Well, is there not a sowing time as well as harvest?" some ask.

Yes, it is true there is; but you can sow with one hand and reap with the other. What would you think of a farmer who went on sowing all the year round and never thought of reaping? I repeat it: We want to sow with one hand and reap with the other, and if we look for the fruit of our labors, we will see it. *"I, if I be lifted up from the earth, will draw all men unto me"* (John 12:32). We must lift Christ up and then seek men out and bring them to Him.

You must use the right kind of bait. A good many don't do this, and then they wonder why they are not successful. You see them getting up all kinds of entertainments with which they try to catch men. They are going about their work the wrong way. This perishing world needs Christ and needs Him crucified. There's a void in every man's bosom that needs to be filled, and if we only approach him with the right kind of bait, we will catch him.

This poor world needs a Savior, and if we are going to be successful in catching men, we must preach Christ crucified—not His life only, but His death also. And if we are only faithful in doing this, we will succeed. Why is that? Because there is His promise: *"Follow me, and I will make you fishers of men."* That promise holds just as good to you and me as it did to His disciples and is as true now as it was in their time.

Think of Paul up yonder. People are going up every day and every hour, men and women who have been brought to Christ through his writings. He set streams in motion that have flowed on for more than a thousand years. I can imagine men going up to heaven and saying, "Paul, I thank you for writing that letter to the Ephesians; I found Christ in that." "Paul, I thank you for writing that epistle to the Corinthians." "Paul, I found Christ in that epistle to the Philippians." "Thank you, Paul, for that epistle to the Galatians; I found Christ in that." And so, I suppose, they are going up still, thanking Paul all the while for what he did.

Ah, when Paul was put in prison, he did not fold his hands and sit down in idleness! No, he began to write, and his epistles have come down through the long ages of time and brought thousands on thousands to a knowledge of Christ crucified. Yes, Christ told Paul he would be a fisher of men if he followed Him, and he has been fishing for souls ever since. The devil thought he had done a very wise thing when he got Paul into prison, but he was very much mistaken. He overdid it, for once. I have no doubt Paul has thanked God ever since for that Philippian jail and his stripes and imprisonment there. I am sure the world has made more by it than we will ever know until we get to heaven.

The "I Will" of Comfort

The next "I will" is John 14:18: *"I will not leave you comfortless: I will come to you."*

To me, it is a sweet thought that Christ has not left us alone in the dark wilderness here below. Although He has gone up on high and taken His seat by the Father's throne, He has not left us comfortless. A better translation is, "I will not leave you orphans." He did not leave Joseph when they cast him into prison: *"God was with him"* (Acts 7:9). When Daniel was cast into the den of lions, they had to put the Almighty in with him. They were so bound together that they could not be separated, and so God went down into the den of lions with Daniel.

If we have Christ with us, we can do all things. (See Philippians 3:14.) Let us not be thinking how weak we are. Let us lift up our eyes to Him and think of Him as our Elder Brother who has all power given to Him in heaven and on earth. He says, *"Lo, I am with you alway, even unto the end of the world"* (Matthew 28:20). Some of our children and friends leave us, and it is a very sad hour. But, thank God, the believer and Christ will never be separated!

Christ is with us here, and we will be with Him in person by and by and will see Him in His beauty. Not only is He with us, but He has sent us the Holy Spirit. Let us honor the

Holy Spirit by acknowledging that He is here in our midst. He has power to give sight to the blind, to give liberty to the captive, and to open the ears of the deaf that they may hear the glorious words of the Gospel.

The "I Will" of Resurrection

There is another "I will" in John, and it occurs four times in some form in chapter six: *"I will raise him up at the last day"* (John 6:40, 44, 54; see John 6:39).

I rejoice to think that I have a Savior who has power over death. My blessed Master holds the keys to death and hell. I pity the poor unbeliever and the infidel because they have no hope in the resurrection. But every child of God can open that chapter and read the promise, and his heart ought to leap within him for joy as he reads it.

You know the tradesman generally puts the best specimen of his wares in the window to show us the quality of his stock. And so, when Christ was down here, He gave us a specimen of what He could do. He raised three from the dead so that we might know what power He had. There was Jairus's daughter, the widow's son, and Lazarus of Bethany. He raised all three of them so that every doubt might be swept away from our hearts.

How dark and gloomy this world would be if we had no hope in the resurrection; but now, when we lay our little children down in the grave, although it is in sorrow, it is not without hope. We have seen them pass away, we have seen them in the terrible struggle with death; but there has been one star to illuminate the darkness and gloom—the thought that though the happy circle has been broken on earth, it will be completed again in yonder world of heavenly light.

You who have lost a loved one, rejoice as you read this "I will"! Those who have died in Christ will come forth again, by and by. The darkness will flee away, and the morning light of the resurrection will dawn upon us. It is only a little while, and He, whose voice will be heard in the grave, has said it will come: *"I will raise him up at the last day."* Precious promise! Precious "I will"!

I had an unsaved brother for whom I was very anxious. For fourteen long years I tried to lead that brother to *"the Lamb of God, which taketh away the sin of the world"* (John 1:29). My brother was the Benjamin of the family, born a few weeks after my father's death. When he was seventeen, he had a long run of typhoid fever, and he never fully recovered from it.

I did everything I could to bring him to Christ. He was a young man of considerable promise. I know no one who could sit down and discuss against the divinity of Christ like that man. I was not any match for him in argument. Day by day, I preached to him as best I knew how.

I think I never loved a man on earth as I loved that brother. I never knew what it was to love a father because he died before I remember. I loved my brother so much, perhaps because he was sickly, and that drew my love and sympathy toward him. Oh, how my heart yearned for his salvation!

After preaching one night, I said, "Now if any of this audience would like to take up his cross and follow Christ, I would like him to rise," and I cannot tell you what a thrill of joy filled my soul when that brother of mine arose. It seemed the happiest night of my life. I was full of joy and thankfulness, and afterward my brother and I worked together for a time and talked of the Gospel. In the summer we sat upon the hillside and talked about the old home.

After a year had passed, I went to Chicago, and he was to go with me. He bid me goodbye, and I said, "Well, Samuel, I will see you in a few days, and I will only say good-bye until then."

A few days after that, a telegram came, saying, "Samuel is dead." I had to travel a thousand miles to bury him, and I got more comfort out of that promise, *"I will raise him up at the last day"* (John 6:40), than anything else in the Bible. How it cheered me! How it lighted up my path! And as I went into the room and looked upon the lovely face of my brother, how that passage ran through my soul. I said, "Thank God for that promise." It was worth more than the world to me.

When we laid him in the grave, it seemed as if I could hear the voice of Jesus Christ saying, *"Thy brother shall rise again"* (John 11:23). Blessed promise of resurrection! Blessed "I will"! *"I will raise him up at the last day."*

The "I Will" of Glory

Now, the next "I will" is in John 17:24: *"Father, I will that they also, whom thou hast given me, be with me where I am."*

This was in His last prayer in the guest chamber on the last night before He was crucified and died that terrible death on Calvary. Many a believer's countenance begins to light up at the thought that he will see the King in His beauty, by and by. Yes, there is a glorious day before us in the future.

Some think that on the first day we are converted, we have everything. To be sure, we get salvation for the past and peace for the present, but then there is the glory for the future in store. That's what kept Paul rejoicing. He talked of his light afflictions and the mean remarks and stones that were thrown at him, but the glory that was beyond them allowed Paul to count them as nothing: *"I count all things but loss for the excellency of the knowledge of Christ Jesus my Lord... and do count them but dung, that I may win Christ"* (Philippians 3:8).

And so, when things go against us, let us cheer up; let us remember that the night will soon pass away and the morning dawn upon us. Death never comes there. It is banished from that heavenly land. Sickness and pain and sorrow do not come there to mar that grand and glorious home where we will be by and by with the Master. God's family will be all together there.

Glorious future, my friends! Yes, glorious days, and it may be a great deal nearer than many of us think. During these few days we are here, let us stand steadfast and firm, and by and by we will be in the unbroken circle in the yonder world of light and have the King in our midst.

About the Author

Dwight Lyman Moody

(1837–1899)

On February 5, 1837, in Northfield, Massachusetts, Dwight Lyman Moody was born, the sixth in what would be a family of nine children. His father died when Moody was only a tender child, leaving little provision for the family. Thus, Moody learned the value of hard work at an early age. An ambitious Moody went to Boston at the age of seventeen, where he became a successful salesman in his uncle's shoe store. His uncle made him promise to go to church, a promise that he faithfully kept, and he was won to the Lord by his Sunday-school teacher.

In 1856, Moody went to Chicago, where he continued to succeed as a shoe salesman. His fervor in selling shoes was exceeded, however, by his zeal in winning souls, and he began to pack the pews of the church with young men.

At the age of twenty-three, he devoted himself to full-time Christian work. Because of his poor grammar, his first attempts at public speaking were not well received by all: one deacon told him that he would serve God best by keeping still.

Nonetheless, Moody persevered, and he became famous nationwide for his Sunday-school work. He was also known for his ministry to the soldiers during the Civil War; many were brought to Christ through his meetings and through his distribution of Bibles and tracts.

In 1867, Moody traveled to Great Britain to learn new methods in Christian work. It was there that his heart was stirred and forever changed by these words, spoken to him by a well-known evangelist: "The world has yet to see what God will do with…the man who is fully consecrated to Him." Moody determined to be that man.

The road of full commitment was not without trials. In 1871, the church that Moody pastored, the largest church in Chicago, was destroyed in the Chicago fire. But in the wake of this disaster, Moody received the filling of the Holy Spirit. Never before had he experienced such a mighty revelation of God's love.

After this empowering of the Spirit, Moody went on to accomplish even more for Christ. He held meetings in America, England, and Scotland, where thousands were in attendance and many were brought to Christ, and founded Moody Bible Institute.

When Moody died in 1899, he left a rich legacy: three Christian schools, a Christian publishing business, and a million souls won for Christ. The day of his death was not a sad day; rather, Moody exclaimed, "This is my triumph; this is my coronation day!"

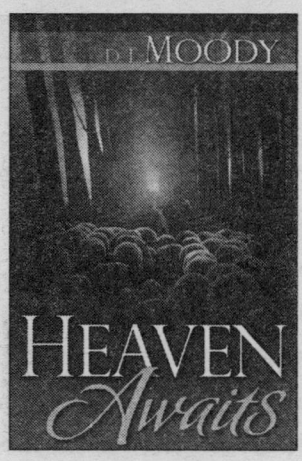

Heaven Awaits
D. L. Moody

"How can I get to heaven?"

This question is asked by millions of people today. Help, encouragement, and definite answers await the reader, as page after page unfolds with the explanation of this exciting place—heaven—and how we can get there. With tremendous insight, D. L. Moody, a dynamic evangelist who reached thousands of people throughout the world with his special message of Christ's love, offers easy to understand explanations that make this book one that must be read and shared with others.

ISBN: 978-1-60374-036-4 • Pocket • 160 pages

www.whitakerhouse.com

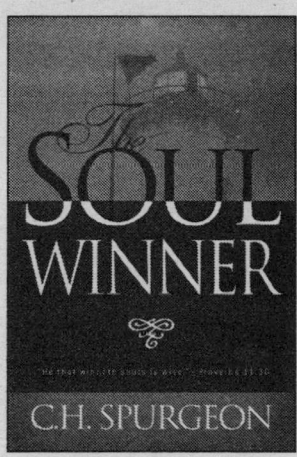

The Soulwinner
Charles H. Spurgeon

When Jesus returned to heaven, He left us with a mission—continue His work of bringing lost souls home to the Father. Charles Spurgeon accepted this mission and personally escorted thousands of people into the saving knowledge of Jesus Christ. In this book, he crystallizes the wisdom and experience of a lifetime as a soulwinner.

"If you are eager for real joy, I am persuaded that no joy of growing wealthy, no joy of influence over your fellow creatures, no joy of any other sort, can ever compare with the rapture of saving a soul from death."
—C. H. Spurgeon

ISBN: 978-0-88368-709-3 • Trade • 304 pages

www.whitakerhouse.com

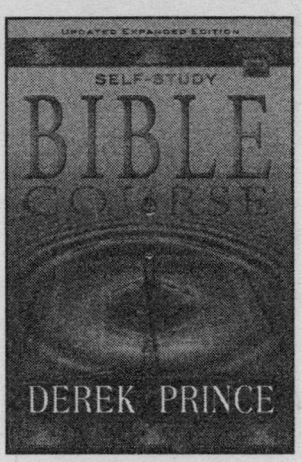

Self-Study Bible Course
Updated & Expanded Edition
Derek Prince

If you have questions about God and the Bible, here is help for you. In this newly updated and expanded self-study course by internationally recognized Bible teacher Derek Prince, you will find answers to questions such as, "How can I have victory over sin?" and "How can I receive answers to my prayers?" Through this study, you will experience important changes in your life and discover an intimacy with God that you may have never known before.

ISBN: 978-0-88368-750-5 • Workbook • 216 pages

www.whitakerhouse.com